READING
Between the Lines

Fiction and Poetry
Texts that Imagine, Explore and Entertain

Published by Letts Educational
The Chiswick Centre
414 Chiswick High Road
London W4 5TF
☎ 020 89963333
📠 020 89968390
✉ mail@lettsed.co.uk
🌐 www.letts-education.com

Letts Educational Limited is a division of
Granada Learning Limited, part of the Granada
Media Group.

ISBN 1840855770

British Library Cataloguing in Publication Data
A catalogue record for this book is available
from the British Library.

Project editors: Jo Sherbourne, Jo Kemp
Illustration: Julia Bickham
Editorial, design and production: Topics –
The Creative Partnership, Exeter

Printed and bound in the UK

READING
Between the Lines

Fiction and Poetry
Texts that Imagine, Explore and Entertain

Contents

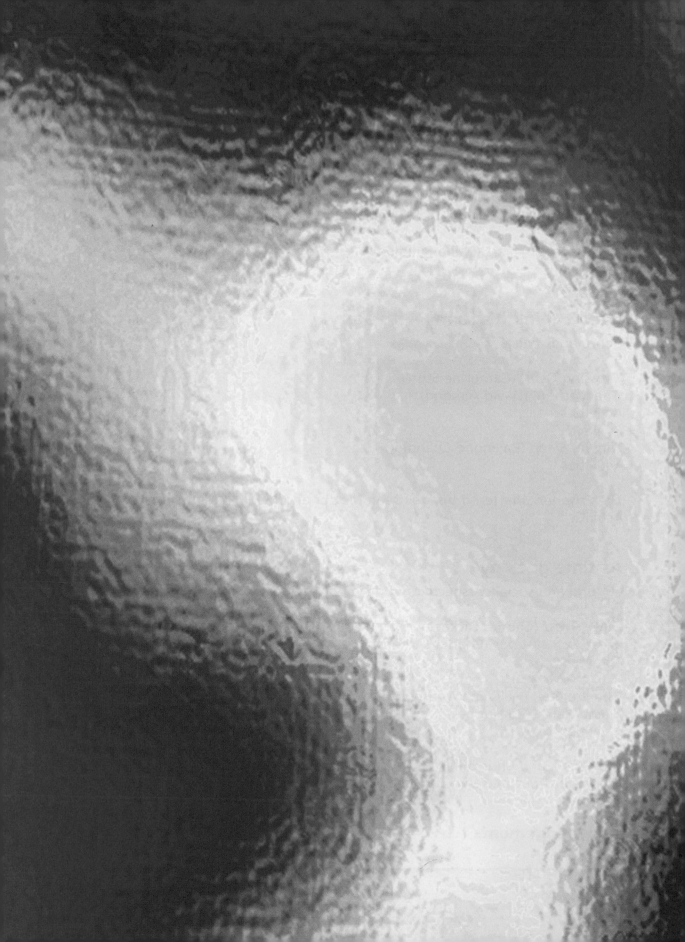

Students' notes

Welcome to a Key Stage 3 anthology. What's an anthology? Well, this one has lots of different texts. Extracts from stories, plays and poems which you may be familiar with, and some you may never have heard of but which may just catch your interest enough for you to investigate further.

In fact, 'investigate' is a key word because cunningly designed activities have been sprinkled liberally throughout the book to help you develop and practise those skills you have achieved with all the hard work you put into your Key Stage 2 Literacy Hours. OK, there may have been a few bad days, a few moments of doubt, but they can't have been all bad because here you are in a Key Stage 3 English lesson about to enjoy reading and working on one of the texts. You may be doing this on your own or with a group, or maybe the whole class is trying to share a limited number of copies; whichever way you have been organised, there is so much in here that something is bound to catch your interest at some time.

That is also another key word – 'time'. As your experience of Key Stage 3 English will be part of your life throughout Years 7, 8 and 9, you may find that you're using this anthology again in a different year because it has been written to include activities for all years at Key Stage 3.

The activities in the **Read, Think and Write** and the **Read and Analyse** sections will help you understand the texts and develop your vocabulary, grammar and writing skills. The **Read, Discuss and Act** section will give you a chance to talk about and act out issues that arise from the text.

The extracts provide examples of the different ways in which writers begin their stories, describe and develop characters, and use language to create particular effects. By using examples of writers' work as models, the anthology may help you develop your own writing skills and your ability to express and communicate your own ideas. It may also inspire you to read more of these writers' work.

I hope the book provides you with some moments you enjoy.

Teacher's notes

The aim of the anthology is to provide a wide variety of texts which could be used for individual study, group reading activities or whole class interaction. An anthology is by its very nature something to dip into, so it has been designed to offer a good measure of flexibility.

There is some differentiation in the way it is organised to enable teachers to plan their work. Each of the five sections contains texts and activities suitable for Year 7 through to Year 9. Some of the texts are whole stories or poems but the majority are extracts of a more sustained length in order to help students develop and practise the skills of analysis they will have experienced with short sections of text in their Key Stage 2 Literacy work. It is also intended to lead them towards the demands of the texts they will work with at Key Stage 4.

The focus or theme of each section is based on the learning objectives of the Key Stage 3 Literacy Framework. The anthology provides students with opportunities to

• explore aspects of story structure;

• investigate how character and motivation are portrayed through description, dialogue and action;

• identify actions, processes and ideas and how writers develop them;

• consider how writers use language structure and style to create particular effects;

• identify the characteristics, style and preoccupations of individual writers from different cultures and times;

- understand the way poets from different times have used sound, imagery and form to evoke meaning, thought or emotion.

The activities have been grouped into three sections and again, to enable planning, each section is focused on the learning objectives of the Key Stage 3 Literacy Framework. The **Read, Think and Write** section contains activities to support a student's grasp of meaning within a text and follows the objectives of the Text level Reading and Writing element of the Literacy Framework. The activities in the **Read and Analyse** section enable a student to practise and develop Word level and Sentence level work. The final section, **Read, Discuss and Act**, provides questions for discussion and drama activities which will ensure that students experience some of the Speaking and Listening objectives in the Framework.

As with all key stages, the spectrum of ability and interest at Key Stage 3 is wide, but the flexibility of this anthology in its choice of texts and the organisation of its activities will enable it to be fitted into a school's English curriculum to provide a stimulating and literacy-focused resource.

Harry Potter and the Chamber of Secrets

by J. K. Rowling

The Dark is Rising

by Susan Cooper

Harry Potter is a character who has appeared in a very popular series of books. This is the opening chapter to a continuation of his adventures. What problems might an author have in beginning a story when the main character has already been introduced in an earlier book?

Susan Cooper's book is also one of a series. Both stories deal with themes associated with the forces of good and evil magic, but in very different ways. Think about how the writers achieve their effects through the characters they introduce.

Harry Potter and the Chamber of Secrets

The Worst Birthday

Not for the first time, an argument had broken out over breakfast at number four, Privet Drive. Mr Vernon Dursley had been woken in the early hours of the morning by a loud hooting noise from his nephew Harry's room.

'Third time this week!' he roared across the table. 'If you can't control that owl, it'll have to go!'

Harry tried, yet again, to explain.

'She's *bored*,' he said. 'She's used to flying around outside. If I could just let her out at night ... '

'Do I look stupid?' snarled Uncle Vernon, a bit of fried egg dangling from his bushy moustache. 'I know what'll happen if that owl's let out.'

He exchanged dark looks with his wife, Petunia.

Harry tried to argue back but his words were drowned by a long, loud belch from the Dursleys' son, Dudley.

'I want more bacon.'

'There's more in the frying pan, sweetums,' said Aunt Petunia, turning misty eyes on her massive son. 'We must feed you up while we've got the chance ... I don't like the sound of that school food ...'

'Nonsense, Petunia, I never went hungry when *I* was at Smeltings,' said Uncle Vernon heartily. 'Dudley gets enough, don't you, son?'

Dudley, who was so large his bottom drooped over either side of the kitchen chair, grinned and turned to Harry.

'Pass the frying pan.'

'You've forgotten the magic word,' said Harry irritably.

The effect of this simple sentence on the rest of the family was incredible: Dudley gasped and fell off his chair with a crash that shook the whole kitchen; Mrs Dursley gave a small scream and clapped her hands to her mouth; Mr Dursley jumped to his feet, veins throbbing in his temples.

'I meant 'please'!' said Harry quickly. 'I didn't mean–'

'WHAT HAVE I TOLD YOU,' thundered his uncle, spraying spit over the table, 'ABOUT SAYING THE M WORD IN OUR HOUSE?'

'But I–'

'HOW DARE YOU THREATEN DUDLEY!' roared Uncle Vernon, pounding the table with his fist.

'I just–'

'I WARNED YOU! I WILL NOT TOLERATE MENTION OF YOUR ABNORMALITY UNDER THIS ROOF!'

Harry stared from his purple-faced uncle to his pale aunt, who was trying to heave Dudley to his feet.

'All right,' said Harry, '*all right ...*'

Uncle Vernon sat back down, breathing like a winded rhinoceros and watching Harry closely out of the corners of his small, sharp eyes.

Ever since Harry had come home for the summer holidays, Uncle Vernon had been treating him like a bomb that might go off at any moment, because Harry *wasn't* a normal boy. As a matter of fact, he was as not normal as it is possible to be.

Harry Potter was a wizard – a wizard fresh from his first year at Hogwarts School of Witchcraft and Wizardry. And if the Dursleys were unhappy to have him back for the holidays, it was nothing to how Harry felt.

He missed Hogwarts so much it was like having a constant stomach ache. He missed the castle, with its secret passageways and ghosts, his lessons (though perhaps not Snape, the potions master), the post arriving by owl, eating banquets in the Great Hall, sleeping in his four-poster bed in the tower dormitory, visiting the gamekeeper, Hagrid, in his cabin in the grounds next to the forbidden forest and, especially, Quidditch, the most popular sport in the wizarding world (six tall goal-posts, four flying balls and fourteen players on broomsticks).

All Harry's spellbooks, his wand, robes, cauldron and top-of-the-range Nimbus Two Thousand broomstick had been locked in a cupboard under the stairs by Uncle Vernon the instant Harry had come home. What did the Dursleys care if Harry lost his place on the house Quidditch team because he hadn't practised all summer? What was it to the Dursleys if Harry went back to school without any of his homework done? The Dursleys were what wizards called Muggles (not a drop of magical blood in their veins) and as far as they were concerned, having a wizard in the family was a matter of deepest shame. Uncle Vernon had even padlocked Harry's owl, Hedwig, inside her cage, to stop her carrying messages to anyone in the wizarding world.

Harry looked nothing like the rest of the family. Uncle Vernon was large and neckless, with an enormous black moustache; Aunt Petunia was horse-faced and boney; Dudley was blonde, pink and porky. Harry, on the other hand, was small and skinny, with brilliant green eyes and jet black hair that was always untidy. He wore round glasses, and on his forehead was a thin, lightning-shaped scar.

The Dark is Rising

Midwinter's Eve

'Too many!' James shouted, and slammed the door behind him.

'What?' said Will.

'Too many kids in this family, that's what. Just *too many*.' James stood fuming on the landing like a small angry locomotive, then stumped across to the window-seat and stared out at the garden. Will put aside his book and pulled up his legs to make room. 'I could hear all the yelling,' he said, chin on knees.

'Wasn't anything,' James said. 'Just stupid Barbara again. Bossing. Pick up this, don't touch that. And Mary joining in, twitter twitter twitter. You'd think this house was big enough, but there's always *people*.'

They both looked out of the window. The snow lay thin and apologetic over the world. That wide grey sweep was the lawn, with the straggling trees of the orchard still dark beyond; the white squares were the roofs of the garage, the old barn, the rabbit hutches, the chicken coops. Further back there were only the flat fields of Dawsons' Farm, dimly white-striped. All the broad sky was grey, full of more snow that refused to fall. There was no colour anywhere.

'Four days to Christmas,' Will said. 'I wish it would snow properly.'

'And your birthday tomorrow.'

'Mmm.' He had been going to say that too, but it would have been too much like a reminder. And the gift he most wished for on his birthday was something nobody could give him: it was snow, beautiful, deep, blanketing snow, and it never came. At least this year there was the grey sprinkle, better than nothing.

He said, remembering a duty: 'I haven't fed the rabbits yet. Want to come?'

Booted and muffled, they clumped out through the sprawling kitchen. A full symphony orchestra was swelling out of the radio; their eldest sister Gwen was slicing onions and singing; their mother was bent broad-beamed and red-faced over an oven. 'Rabbits!' she shouted, when she caught sight of them. 'And some more hay from the farm!'

'We're going!' Will shouted back. The radio let out a sudden hideous crackle of static as he passed the table. He jumped. Mrs Stanton shrieked, 'Turn that thing DOWN.'

Outdoors, it was suddenly very quiet. Will dipped out a pail of pellets from the bin in the farm-smelling barn, which was not really a barn at all, but a long, low building with a tiled roof, once a stable. They tramped through the thin snow to the row of heavy wooden hutches, leaving dark footmarks on the hard frozen ground.

Opening doors to fill the feed-boxes, Will passed, frowning. Normally the rabbits would be huddled sleepily in corners, only the greedy ones coming twitch-nosed forward to eat. Today they seemed restless and uneasy, rustling to and fro, banging against their wooden walls; one or two even leapt back in alarm when he opened their doors. He came to his favourite rabbit, named Chelsea, and reached in as usual to rub him affectionately behind the ears, but the animal scuffled back away from him and cringed into a corner, the pink-rimmed eyes staring up blank and terrified.

'Hey!' Will said, disturbed. 'Hey James, look at that. What's the matter with him? And all of them?

'They seem all right to me.'

'Well, they don't to me. They're all jumpy. Even Chelsea. Hey, come on, boy –' But it was no good.

'Funny,' James said with mild interest, watching. 'I dare say your hands smell wrong. You must have touched something they don't like. Same as dogs and aniseed, but the other way round.'

'I haven't touched anything. Matter of fact, I'd just washed my hands when I saw you.'

'There you are then,' James said promptly. 'That's the trouble. They've never smelt you clean before. Probably all die of shock.'

'Ha very ha.' Will attacked him, and they scuffled together, grinning, while the empty pail toppled rattling on the hard ground. But when he glanced back as they left, the animals were still moving distractedly, not eating yet, staring after him with those strange frightened wide eyes.

'There might be a fox about again, I suppose,' James said. 'Remind me to tell Mum.' No fox could get at the rabbits, in their sturdy row, but the chickens were more vulnerable; a family of foxes had broken into one of the henhouses the previous winter and carried off six nicely-fattened birds just before marketing-time. Mrs Stanton, who relied on the chicken-money each year to

help pay for eleven Christmas presents, had been so furious she had kept watch afterwards in the cold barn two nights running, but the villains had not come back. Will thought that if he were a fox he would have kept clear too; his mother might be married to a jeweller, but with generations of Buckinghamshire farmers behind her, she was no joke when the old instincts were roused.

Tugging the handcart, a home-made contraption with a bar joining its shafts, he and James made their way down the curve of the overgrown drive and out along the road to Dawsons' Farm. Quickly past the churchyard, its great dark yew trees leaning out over the crumbling wall; more slowly by Rooks' Wood, on the corner of Church Lane. The tall spinney of horse-chestnut trees, raucous with the calling of the rooks and rubbish-roofed with the clutter of their sprawling nests, was one of their familiar places.

'Hark at the rooks! Something's disturbed them.' The harsh irregular chorus was deafening, and when Will looked up at the tree-tops he saw the sky dark with wheeling birds. They flapped and drifted to and fro; there were no flurries of sudden movement, only this clamorous interweaving throng of rooks.

'An owl?'

'They're not chasing anything. Come on, Will, it'll be getting dark soon.'

'That's why it's so odd for the rooks to be in a fuss. They all ought to be roosting by now.' Will turned his head reluctantly down again, but then jumped and clutched his brother's arm, his eye caught by a movement in the darkening lane that led away from the road where they stood. Church Lane: it ran between Rooks' Wood and the churchyard to the tiny local church, and then on to the River Thames.

'Hey!'

'What's up?'

'There's someone over there. Or there was. Looking at us.'

James sighed. 'So what? Just someone out for a walk.'

'No, he wasn't.' Will screwed up his eyes nervously, peering down the little side road. 'It was a weird-looking man all hunched over, and when he saw me looking he ran off behind a tree. *Scuttled*, like a beetle.'

James heaved at the handcart and set off up the road, making Will run to keep up. 'It's just a tramp, then. I dunno, everyone seems to be going batty today – Barb and the rabbits and the rooks and now you, all yak-twitchetty-yakking. Come on, let's get that hay. I want my tea.'

The handcart bumped through the frozen ruts into Dawsons' yard, the great earthen square enclosed by buildings on three sides, and they smelt the familiar farm-smell. The cowshed must have been mucked out that day; Old George, the toothless cattleman, was piling dung across the yard. He raised a hand to them. Nothing missed Old George; he could see a hawk drop from a mile away. Mr Dawson came out of a barn.

'Ah,' he said. 'Hay for Stantons' Farm?' It was his joke with their mother, because of the rabbits and the hens.

James said, 'Yes, please.'

'It's coming,' Mr Dawson said. Old George had disappeared into the barn. 'Keeping well, then? Tell your mum I'll have ten birds off her tomorrow. And four rabbits. Don't look like that, young Will. If it's not their happy Christmas, it's one for the folks as'll have them.' He glanced up at the sky, and Will thought a strange look came over his lined brown face. Up against the lowering grey clouds, two black rooks were flapping slowly over the farm in a wide circle.

'The rooks are making an awful din today,' James said. 'Will saw a tramp up by the wood.'

Mr Dawson looked at Will sharply. 'What was he like?'

'Just a little old man. He dodged away.'

'So the Walker is abroad,' the farmer said softly to himself. 'Ah. He would be.'

'Nasty weather for walking,' James said cheerfully. He nodded at the northern sky over the farmhouse roof; the clouds there seemed to be growing darker, massing in ominous grey mounds with a yellowish tinge. The wind was rising too; it stirred their hair, and they could hear a distant rustling from the tops of the trees.

'More snow coming,' said Mr Dawson.

'It's a horrible day,' said Will suddenly, surprised by his own violence; after all, he had wanted snow. But somehow uneasiness was growing in him. 'It's – creepy, somehow.'

'It will be a bad night,' said Mr Dawson.

'There's Old George with the hay,' said James. 'Come on, Will.'

'You go,' the farmer said. 'I want Will to pick up something for your mother from the house.' But he did not move, as James pushed the handcart off towards the barn; he stood with his hands thrust deep into the pockets of his old tweed jacket, looking at the darkening sky.

'The Walker is abroad,' he said again. 'And this night will be bad, and tomorrow will be beyond imagining.' He looked at Will, and Will looked back in growing alarm into the weathered face, the bright dark eyes creased narrow by decades of peering into sun and rain and wind. He had never noticed before how dark Farmer Dawson's eyes were: strange, in their blue-eyed county.

'You have a birthday coming,' the farmer said.

'Mmm,' said Will.

'I have something for you.' He glanced briefly round the yard, and withdrew one hand from his pocket; in it, Will saw what looked like a kind of ornament, made of black metal, a flat circle quartered by two crossed lines. He took it, fingering it curiously. It was about the size of his palm, and quite heavy; roughly forged out of iron, he guessed, though with no sharp points or edges. The iron was cold to his hand.

'What is it?' he said.

'For the moment,' Mr Dawson said, 'just call it something to keep. To keep with you always, all the time. Put it in your pocket, now. And later on, loop your belt through it and wear it like an extra buckle.'

Will slipped the iron circle into his pocket. 'Thank you very much,' he said, rather shakily. Mr Dawson, usually a comforting man, was not improving the day at all.

The farmer looked at him in the same intent, unnerving way, until Will felt the hair rise on the back of his neck; then he gave a twisted half-smile, with no amusement in it but a kind of anxiety. 'Keep it safe, Will. And the less you happen to talk about it, the better. You will need it after the snow comes.' He became brisk. 'Come on, now, Mrs Dawson has a jar of her mincemeat for your mother.'

They moved off towards the farmhouse. The farmer's wife was not there, but waiting in the doorway was Maggie Barnes, the farm's round-faced, red-cheeked dairymaid, who always reminded Will of an apple. She beamed at them both, holding out a big white crockery jar tied with a red ribbon.

'Thank you, Maggie,' Farmer Dawson said.

'Missus said you'd be wanting it for young Will here,' Maggie said. 'She went down the village to see the vicar for something. How's your big brother, then, Will?'

She always said this, whenever she saw him; she meant Will's next-to-oldest brother Max. It was a Stanton family joke that Maggie Barnes at Dawsons' had a thing about Max.

'Fine, thank you,' Will said politely. 'Grown his hair long. Looks like a girl.'

Maggie shrieked with delight. 'Get away with you!' She giggled and waved her farewell, and just at the last moment Will noticed her gaze slip upward past his head. Out of the corner of his eye as he turned, he thought he saw a flicker of movement by the farmyard gate, as if someone were dodging quickly out of sight. But when he looked, no one was there.

With the big pot of mincemeat wedged between two bales of hay, Will and James pushed the handcart out of the yard. The farmer stood in his doorway behind them; Will could feel his eyes, watching. He glanced up uneasily at the looming, growing clouds, and half-unwillingly slipped a hand into his pocket to finger the strange iron circle. '*After the snow comes.*' The sky looked as if it were about to fall on them. He thought: *what's happening?*

One of the farm dogs came bounding up, tail waving; then it stopped abruptly a few yards away, looking at them.

'Hey, Racer!' Will called.

The dog's tail went down, and it snarled, showing its teeth.

'James!' said Will.

'He won't hurt you. What's the matter?'

They went on, and turned into the road.

'It's not that. Something's wrong, that's all. Something's awful. Racer, Chelsea – the animals are all scared of me.' He was beginning to be really frightened now.

The noise from the rookery was louder, even though the daylight was beginning to die. They could see the dark birds thronging over the treetops, more agitated than before, flapping and turning to and fro. And Will had been right; there was a stranger in the lane, standing beside the churchyard.

He was a shambling, tattered figure, more like a bundle of old clothes than a man, and at the sight of him the boys slowed their pace and drew instinctively closer to the cart and to one another. He turned his shaggy head to look at them.

Then suddenly, in a dreadful blur of unreality, a hoarse, shrieking flurry was rushing dark down out of the sky, and two huge rooks swooped at the man. He staggered back, shouting, his hands thrust up to protect his face, and the birds flapped their great wings in a black vicious whirl and were gone, swooping up past the boys and into the sky.

Will and James stood frozen, staring, pressed against the bales of hay.

The stranger cowered back against the gate.

'Kaaaaaak … kaaaaaak …' came the head-splitting racket from the frenzied flock over the wood, and then three more whirling black shapes were swooping after the first two, diving wildly at the man and then away. This time he screamed in terror and stumbled out into the road, his arms still wrapped in

defence round his head, his face down; and he ran. The boys heard the frightened gasps for breath as he dashed headlong past them, and up the road past the gates of Dawsons' Farm and on towards the village. They saw bushy, greasy grey hair below a dirty old cap; a torn brown overcoat tied with string, and some other garment flapping beneath it; old boots, one with a loose sole that made him kick his leg oddly sideways, half-hopping, as he ran. But they did not see his face.

The high whirling above their heads was dwindling into loops of slow flight, and the rooks began to settle one by one into the trees. They were still talking loudly to one another in a long cawing jumble, but the madness and the violence were not in it now. Dazed, moving his head for the first time, Will felt his cheek brush against something, and putting his hand to his shoulder, he found a long black feather there. He pushed it into his jacket pocket, moving slowly, like someone half-awake.

Together they pushed the loaded cart down the road to the house, and the cawing behind them died to an ominous murmur, like the swollen Thames in spring.

James said at last, 'Rooks don't do that sort of thing. They don't attack people. And they don't come down low when there's not much space. They just don't.'

'No,' Will said. He was still moving in a detached half-dream, not fully aware of anything except a curious vague groping in his mind. In the midst of all the din and the flurry, he had suddenly had a strange feeling stronger than any he had ever known: he had been aware that someone was trying to tell him something, something that had missed him because he could not understand the words. Not words exactly; it had been like a kind of silent shout. But he had not been able to pick up the message, because he had not known how.

'Like not having the radio on the right station,' he said aloud.

'What?' said James, but he wasn't really listening. 'What a thing,' he said. 'I s'pose the tramp must have been trying to catch a rook. And they got wild. He'll be snooping around after the hens and the rabbits, I bet you. Funny he didn't have a gun. Better tell Mum to leave the dogs in the barn tonight.' He chattered amiably on as they reached home and unloaded the hay. Gradually Will realized in amazement that all the shock of the wild, savage attack was running out of James's mind like water, and that in a matter of minutes even the very fact of its happening had gone.

Something had neatly wiped the whole incident from James's memory; something that did not want it reported. Something that knew this would stop Will from reporting it too.

'Here, take Mum's mincemeat,' James said. 'Let's go in before we freeze. The wind's really getting up – good job we hurried back.'

'Yes,' said Will. He felt cold, but it was not from the rising wind. His fingers closed round the iron circle in his pocket and held it tightly. This time, the iron felt warm.

Read, Think and Write

1. What impression does the writer give of Harry and of the Dursley household in the opening conversation in the Harry Potter extract?

2. What impression does the writer give of Will and of the Stanton household in the opening conversation in *The Dark is Rising* extract?

3. What effect does Harry have on the family by using the word 'magic'?

4. What effect does Will have on the rabbits that he goes to feed? What reason does his brother James give for the rabbits' behaviour?

5. Why does Harry go to a special school? What are some of the things he misses about school?

6. Make a list of the nouns used in the opening of the Harry Potter story which show that the story will involve the use of magical powers.

7. Make a list of the events described in the opening of *The Dark is Rising* which show that the story may involve magical powers.

8. How does the writer describe the appearance of each member of the Dursley family?

9. What is special about Harry Potter's appearance?

10. How does Susan Cooper describe the appearance of 'the stranger in the lane' before and after the attack by the rooks?

11. What effect does the attack on the stranger have on Will and his brother James?

12. Which of the two openings to a story about a 'magical world' do you prefer and why?

Read and Analyse

1. The use of adverbs with the word 'said' or the use of a different speech verb can help the reader understand how the characters are feeling.

   (a) Look closely at what each character says in the opening part of the Harry Potter story and write down what they say when the author uses an adverb to indicate how they speak. Underline the adverb.

   > **Example**
   > 'Nonsense, Petunia, I never went hungry when I was at Smeltings,' said Uncle Vernon <u>heartily</u>.

   (b) Write sentences of your own using these adverbs.

2. Writers often use dialogue to open a story. Write the opening to a story where a family is about to embark on a journey. Use the dialogue between the characters to show what is happening now and what may happen in the future. You might also want your characters to refer to something that has happened in the past. Try to construct sentences that reveal something about the character of the person speaking. (Remember to start a new line when each character speaks.)

   Look at the first part of the Harry Potter extract and use it as a model for your own writing.

Read, Discuss and Act

1. How would you define the word 'magic'? What other stories, or television programmes or films, do you know that have used magic as a theme? Is the word 'magic' used in other contexts? Use a dictionary to check definitions of the word in order to help your discussion.

2. Act out a scene where an old wizard is trying to teach a young magician some new spells.

3. Role-play a family discussion at breakfast time about an event they are planning. It could be a celebration like a birthday party or a holiday. You could use Mr and Mrs Dursley, Dudley and Harry as role models for your family. Read the text to see how each of them behaves to help you with ideas for your own characters.

Holes

by Louis Sachar

These are the opening pages of the story of Stanley Yelnats, a character who comes from a family with a history of bad luck. As you read, think about how the author creates an appropriate atmosphere in which to develop a plot set in a boys' juvenile detention centre.

1

There is no lake at Camp Green Lake. There once was a very large lake here, the largest lake in Texas. That was over a hundred years ago. Now it is just a dry flat wasteland.

There used to be a town of Green Lake as well. The town shriveled and dried up along with the lake, and the people who lived there.

During the summer the daytime temperature hovers around ninety-five in the shade – if you can find any shade. There's not much shade in a big dry lake.

The only trees are two old oaks on the eastern edge of the "lake." A hammock is stretched between the two trees, and a log cabin stands behind that.

The campers are forbidden to lie in the hammock. I belongs to the Warden. The Warden owns the shade.

Out on the lake, rattlesnakes and scorpions find shade under rocks and in the holes dug by the campers.

Here's a good rule to remember about rattlesnakes and scorpions: If you don't bother them, they won't bother you.

Usually.

Being bitten by a scorpion or even a rattlesnake is not the worst thing that can happen to you. You won't die.

Usually.

Sometimes a camper will try to be bitten by a scorpion, or even a small rattlesnake. Then he will get to spend a day or two recovering in his tent, instead of having to dig a hole out on the lake.

But you don't want to be bitten by a yellow-spotted lizard. That's the worst thing that can happen to you. You will die a slow and painful death.

Always.

If you get bitten by a yellow-spotted lizard, you might as well go into the shade of the oak trees and lie in the hammock.

There is nothing anyone can do to you anymore.

2

The reader is probably asking: Why would anyone go to Camp Green Lake?

Most campers weren't given a choice. Camp Green Lake is a camp for bad boys.

If you take a bad boy and make him dig a hole every day in the hot sun, it will turn him into a good boy.

That was what some people thought.

Stanley Yelnats was given a choice. The judge said, "You may go to jail, or you may go to Camp Green Lake."

Stanley was from a poor family. He had never been to camp before.

3

Stanley Yelnats was the only passenger on the bus, not counting the driver or the guard. The guard sat next to the driver with his seat turned around facing Stanley. A rifle lay across his lap.

Stanley was sitting about ten rows back, handcuffed to his armrest. His backpack lay on the seat next to him. It contained his toothbrush, toothpaste, and a box of stationery his mother had given him. He'd promised to write to her at least once a week.

He looked out the window, although there wasn't much to see – mostly fields of hay and cotton. He was on a long bus ride to nowhere. The bus wasn't air-conditioned, and the hot, heavy air was almost as stifling as the handcuffs.

Stanley and his parents had tried to pretend that he was just going away to camp for a while, just like rich kids do. When Stanley was younger he used to play with stuffed animals, and pretend the animals were at camp. Camp Fun and Games he called it. Sometimes he'd have them play soccer with a marble. Other times they'd run an obstacle course, or go bungee jumping off a table, tied to broken rubber bands. Now Stanley tried to pretend he was going to Camp Fun and Games. Maybe he'd make some friends, he thought. At least he'd get to swim in the lake.

He didn't have any friends at home. He was overweight and the bids at his middle school often teased him about his size. Even his teachers sometimes made cruel comments without realizing it. On his last day of school, his math teacher, Mrs. Bell, taught ratios. As an example, she chose the heaviest kid in the class and the lightest kid in the class, and had them weigh themselves. Stanley weighed three times as much as the other boy. Mrs. Bell wrote the ratio on the board, 3:1, unaware of how much embarrassment she had caused both of them.

Stanley was arrested later that day.

He looked at the guard who sat slumped in his seat and wondered if he had fallen asleep. The guard was wearing sunglasses, so Stanley couldn't see his eyes.

Stanley was not a bad kid. He was innocent of the crime for which he was convicted. He'd just been in the wrong place at the wrong time.

It was all because of his no-good-dirty-rotten-pig-stealing-great-great-grandfather!

He smiled. It was a family joke. Whenever anything went wrong, they always blamed Stanley's no-good-dirty-rotten-pig-stealing-great-great-grandfather.

Supposedly, he had a great-great-grandfather who stolen a pig from a long-legged Gypsy, and she put a curse on him and all his descendants. Stanley and his parents didn't believe in curses, of course, but whenever anything went wrong, it felt good to be able to blame someone.

Things went wrong a lot. They always seemed to be in the wrong place at the wrong time.

He looked out the window at the vast emptiness. He watched the rise and fall of a telephone wire. In his mind he could hear his father's gruff voice softly singing to him.

"If only, if only," the woodpecker sighs,
"The bark on the tree was just a little bit softer."
While the wolf waits below, hungry and lonely,
He cries to the moo—oo—oon,
"If only, if only."

It was a song his father used to sing to him. The melody was sweet and sad, but Stanley's favorite part was when his father would howl the word "moon."

The bus hit a small bump and the guard sat up, instantly alert.

Stanley's father was an inventor. To be a successful inventor you need three things: intelligence, perseverance, and just a little bit of luck.

Stanley's father was smart and had a lot of perseverance. Once he started a project he would work on it for years, often going days without sleep. He just never had any luck.

Every time an experiment failed, Stanley could hear him cursing his dirty-rotten-pig-stealing-great-grandfather.

Stanley's father was also named Stanley Yelnats. Stanley's father's full name was Stanley Yelnats III. Our Stanley is Stanley Yelnats IV.

Everyone in his family had always like the fact that "Stanley Yelnats" was spelled the same frontward and backward. So they kept naming their sons Stanley. Stanley was an only child, as was every other Stanley Yelnats before him.

All of them had something else in common. Despite their awful luck, they always remained hopeful. As Stanley's father liked to say, "I learn from failure."

But perhaps that was part of the curse as well. If Stanley and his father weren't always hopeful, then it wouldn't hurt so much every time their hopes were crushed.

"Not every Stanley Yelnats has been a failure," Stanley's mother often pointed out, whenever Stanley or his father became so discouraged that they actually started to believe in the curse. The first Stanley Yelnats, Stanley's great-grandfather, had made a fortune in the stock market. "He couldn't have been too unlucky."

At such times she neglected to mention the bad luck that befell the first Stanley Yelnats. He lost his entire fortune when he was moving from New York to California. His stagecoach was robbed by the outlaw Kissin' Kate Barlow.

If it weren't for that, Stanley's family would now be living in a mansion on a beach in California. Instead, they were carmmed in a tiny apartment that smelled of burning rubber and foot odor.

If only, if only …

The apartment smelled the way it did because Stanley's father was trying to invent a way to recycle old sneakers. "The first person who finds a use for old sneakers," he said, "will be a very rich man."

It was this latest project that led to Stanley's arrest.

The bus ride became increasingly bumpy because the road was no longer paved.

Actually, Stanley had been impressed when he first found out that his great-grandfather was robbed by Kissin' Kate Barlow. True, he would have preferred living on the beach in California, but it was still kind of cool to have someone in your family robbed by a famous outlaw.

Kate Barlow didn't actually kiss Stanley's great-grandfather. That would have been really cool, but she only kissed the men she killed. Instead, she robbed him and left him stranded in the middle of the desert.

"He was *lucky* to have survived," Stanley's mother was quick to point out.

The bus was slowing down. The guard grunted as he stretched his arms.

"Welcome to Camp Green Lake," said the driver.

Stanley looked out the dirty window. He couldn't see a lake.

And hardly anything was green.

25

Read, Think and Write

1. In the first three paragraphs, the writer immediately describes Camp Green Lake in a negative and rather threatening way. Give three reasons why this is not a good place to be.

2. The first character introduced is also seen as threatening. Who is the character and how does the writer convey this impression?

3. How does the writer make the rest of the first chapter increasingly menacing?

4. How does the first sentence of Chapter 2 link with the ideas in Chapter 1?

5. How does the writer continue to build up a negative and bleak picture of Camp Green Lake in Chapter 2?

6. Who is the character introduced in Chapter 2 and how does the writer make him seem the opposite of the character mentioned in Chapter 1?

7. Chapter 3 shifts the setting. Who are the characters mentioned at the opening of this chapter and where are they?

8. How had Stanley and his parents coped with the idea of him 'going away to camp'?

9. What happened to Stanley on his last day of school?

10. What is unusual about Stanley Yelnats' name?

11. 'Things went wrong a lot.' How is the negative theme of failure continued by what we learn about Stanley and his family?

12. 'Despite their awful luck, they always remained hopeful.' How is the positive theme of hopefulness shown by what we learn about Stanley and his family?

13. 'It was all because of his no-good-dirty-rotten-pig-stealing-great-great-grandfather!' This expression is repeated as a consolation for things not going to plan. Find two other examples where repetition is used to emphasise how things could have been different.

14. The writer has left some unanswered questions in the opening of this story. What do we still need to know about: (a) Stanley; (b) Camp Green Lake?

1. The writer uses very short chapters to open this story. The paragraphs are also very short in Chapters 1 and 2. Look through the text. Where does the writer use single sentence paragraphs? What effect is achieved by doing this?

2. Paragraphing helps to structure and organise ideas. Longer paragraphs are constructed by giving more detail to a main idea. Look at the first five paragraphs of Chapter 3 and pick out the main idea from each of them.

3. Using information from the text to help you develop the detail, write a paragraph about each of the following main ideas:
(a) Stanley's journey on the bus;
(b) Stanley's father;
(c) Stanley's attitude to his great-great-grandfather.

4. Despite Stanley's attempts to remain <u>hopeful</u>, the opening of the story presents an opposing <u>hopeless</u> situation. Find an antonym for these <u>negative</u> words from the text:

Write a sentence for each of the <u>positive</u> words.

Hint
Use a thesaurus.

1. Although Stanley is heading towards a 'bad' environment, he is not a 'bad' boy. Why was Stanley arrested? The opening only gives clues. It says that he was 'in the wrong place at the wrong time'.

Work in a small group to develop the court scene where Stanley tries to explain what happened. You could introduce other characters and let them give their point of view. For example, Stanley's father might explain how it was his latest project that led to Stanley being wrongly accused. In opposition to the positive points of the discussion from Stanley and his father, you will need to introduce the view of a more negative character who is convinced that Stanley is guilty.

Forever X

by Geraldine McCaughrean

This extract is the opening two chapters of a story which uses a 'themed' hotel as a setting for an inventive and thought-provoking plot. As you read, think about how the author has used the characters and setting to introduce and develop the 'theme'.

1
Snow

There was a thud, and Joy woke to the impression that it was snowing. A blizzard of white flurried past the car window. This was odd, given the sweat crawling down inside her T-shirt. It recalled to mind illness, feverishness, hallucinations.

'Damn,' said her father.

'What happened?'

'Fancy a seagull, this far from the sea,' said her mother.

It was August and ninety degrees in the shade. Mr Shepherd had hit a seagull and holed the radiator. Shortly afterwards, the car began to overheat, so that steam drifted past the windows like dense winter fog.

All along the motorway they had been passing broken-down cars and vans and motorcaravans, their passengers spilled out on to the hard shoulder. Mr Shepherd had small hopes of getting a breakdown vehicle without a wait of several hours, and Mrs Shepherd had heard that the hard shoulder of a motorway was the single most dangerous place in the entire universe. So they struck off cross-country at the next exit, looking for a garage, and found themselves among the tarns and fells of the Lake District.

'We might just not get to Linstock tonight,' warned Dad. 'We may have to stay over somewhere here.'

No one in the car said anything. No one dared to speak the treachery of what they were thinking. Each summer the Shepherd family spent their annual holiday in Linstock, in a caravan in the back garden of Gran and Grandpa Shepherd's semi. Joy was of the opinion they could all just as easily stay home and shut themselves in the fridge, and save on petrol. But she only thought. To say so out loud would have been disloyal. Even though everyone was thinking the same. Every summer without fail they spent two weeks in that caravan. Only twenty miles from the sea, it was, and right under the motorway.

Perhaps the car picked up on all their unspoken yearnings *not* to reach Linstock and that caravan. For all of a sudden it stopped. There was no garage within sight, no telephone, no roadside houses, nothing – only a long purple valley and a lake scrawled on, like pale blue paper, by whole sentences of ducks, punctuated with moorhens and exclamations of sunlight.

Jack Shepherd rolled the car into a farm gateway, safely off the road, and everyone stood around it, helpless, marooned. Only Mel went on sleeping, sprawled across his mother's shoulder. Little children could sleep through the End of the World.

There was no gate to the farm track, only a cattle grid, and beside it – like a blessed sign from God in the wilderness – a wooden door-panel painted with the words '*B & B/Full Board*' and a snowflake.

'That's it, then,' said Mr Shepherd nodding at the sign. 'Don't let's leave anything in the car.'

He never left anything in the car, assuming that car thieves dogged his tracks with gleaming eyes and wolfish resolve to strip the Fiesta bare. So he heaved all the suitcases out now and, with his wife carrying Mel, led his family off along the track towards the promise of bed-and-breakfast.

Broad and dusty, the cart-track climbed the fellside steadily, coiling round the hill, round and up, the view gradually growing into larger and larger vistas of deep grass, tumbling scree, sky-filled lake, sunbleached rocks. They passed an electrical substation humming like the distant, unseen motorway, way, way off. The air was dense, breezeless, and had to be waded through, as though in the heat it had thickened like gravy. Flies and midges circled over rabbit and sheep droppings, the only movement in a landscape too hot to move.

'I'm thirsty,' said Joy. 'Will they have something to drink? What if they're full? What if they're away on holiday?' Questions rose like larks out of the ground, but it was too hot for anyone to bother answering them.

Suddenly Mr Shepherd shouted, 'Mind yourselves!' and a slab of metal and glass hurtled down on them trailing dust: a 42-seater coach, empty but for its driver.

Seeing pedestrians on the path, the driver slowed the coach to a crunching skid, nodded his red-cheeked head at them. 'All right?' he called brightly.

Mr Shepherd opened his mouth to answer, but the coach driver, stirring his way through the gears, put his foot down and sped away like a glossy mirage.

'I bet he scrapes the car,' said father looking disconsolately back down the track.

Even so, in a landscape worryingly untouched by the twentieth century, the coach was a hopeful sign. The Shepherds righted their wheel-along suitcases and hauled them round the next bend in the everlasting track.

And there it was – a large white building, its brown lawn marked out by miniature pine trees, a gravel car park as streaked with oil as an English beach, a black tin barn. Mel woke and was instantly delighted. 'A donkey!' he said.

Anne Shepherd looked her children over and tweaked at their damp, dark hair and her own, hoping to present a good impression. But in the light of the sweaty T-shirts, the dusty trainers, the chocolate stains, she instructed everyone to look as appealing as possible.

Abandoning the suitcases, they crowded into the square of shade beneath the porch. 'You're duly warned,' said their mother crisply, 'I shall cry if we're turned away.' Jack Shepherd knocked.

As they waited, Joy let her eyes run idly over the house. The names of the proprietors were written across the lintel: *Licensed for the sale of … Props: Colin and Ivy Partridge.* There was an English Tourist Board car sticker in the glass of the front door, and each pane had white sediment in one corner. Despite the bright sunlight, at this close range, Joy could see now that a string of dirt-caked, dislodged light bulbs snaked to and fro beside the porch. By turning her head sideways she could just make out that the bulbs formed letters, words: FOREVER X. A further group of unlit bulbs had clumped together underneath, like purple grapes left to wither on the vine.

There was music playing indoors – loud laughter and a man's voice. The laughter gained momentum as it came towards them, and thudded heavily against the far side of the door. Their knocking must have gone unheard, for

the man who opened up was not expecting to find anyone on the step. He was elderly, with wild white hair and a beard hooked on over his ears. Thanks to this stifling gag of nylon wool, the thick, red, high-necked jacket, red trousers, wellington boots, and scarlet mittens, his face was an apoplectic smudge of melting purple, his eyes bulging and wide. At the sight of strangers blocking his way, he reeled and gave an inarticulate grunt. Then, recovering himself, he bared at them a fine set of porcelain dentures, and began to nod and laugh and laugh and nod. 'Eeh, grand,' he said. 'Just grand!' A shaking hand reached out to chuck Mel under the chin, then the old man lunged through, scattering the Shepherds off the doormat, and made for the barn, head down saying, 'Merry Christmas! Merry Christmas, one and all, yes.' Mel stared after him, eyes wide, silenced by ecstasy and bewilderment.

'Have you booked?' Catching sight of the Shepherds as she hurried between dining room and kitchen, a woman came to the door, picking up a desk diary from the hall table as she came.

'We broke down,' said Mr Shepherd, off balance. 'The car.'

'Do you by any chance have a vacancy for tonight?' said his wife appealingly. 'Absolutely anything would do!'

'It's tea time,' said Ivy Partridge, shrilly accusing. And then, 'You'd best come in. I'll have to finish off the old ladies first.' As she opened the door to the dining room, not a muscle of her face flinched from a fusillade of gunshots. Joy deduced afterwards that the noise must have been crackers.

The Shepherds waited, mesmerized by the sight and ting-ting-tinging of angel chimes spinning above four lighted candles on the hall table. Somewhere under the stairs, Bing Crosby was singing, though to a different beat.

When Mrs Partridge returned, she thrust a plate of hot mince pies under their noses. 'It's all right,' she said with a fleeting smile, 'I've set the Queen's Speech going. That should keep them happy for ten minutes. I'll show you up.' And she led the way to a large family bedroom.

An octopus of paper-chains hung between the centre lampshade and the picture rails. Tinsel garlands sagged in swags from bedpost to bedpost, while pop-up paper Santas pinned to the wall thrust out concertina bellies which had faded to pink in the brilliant sunshine. Behind the door, above the Fire Notice, a letter-heading had been taped to the wall. It said: *FOREVER XMAS: Christmas comes but once a year … except with us!*

'You'll not be stopping, then?' said Mrs Partridge. 'Just the one night, is it?' The Shepherds stood stranded in the narrow channels between the archipelago of beds, staring around them at prints of flying reindeer. 'Welcome to Forever Xmas. Supper's seven o'clock sharp. Tonight's Monopoly, and the video is *Miracle on 42nd Street*. I wouldn't leave your suitcases in the yard if I were you; coach might run them over when he comes back from pub. Happy Christmas and God bless us every one.'

Dropping the room key on the glass-topped dressing table, she straightened a felt stocking handing from a drawer-knob, then hurried back along the corridor.

'Er … Excuse me … I wonder … please?' called Mrs Shepherd nervously after her. 'Is this … er … I mean to say … Is the Christmas bit obligatory?'

The hinge on the fire-door wheezed like a man punched in the stomach. 'I don't do *vegetarian*, if that's what you mean,' retorted Mrs Partridge and hurried back downstairs before the Queen could finish addressing the nation.

2
Turkeys

What a bonus! What a treat! To walk up a lane and find Christmas at the end of it! Joy prepared to be elated. As she watched Mel run from snow-caked window to tinselled toilet cistern, bouncing off the furniture like a ball in a pinball machine, she prepared to be, like him, entranced. And yet the situation was more odd than wonderful.

She looked to her parents for a clue, a cue: was it really Christmas all year round here? Had they stumbled on some portal in the space/time continuum which would grant them a summertime bite of the Christmas pie? The smells were right: the whole hotel reeked of roasting turkey and boiling pudding. The colours were right – everything red and green, from the carpets to the crockery. And yet. Outside the sun blazed down on Cold Pike until it vibrated like a white-hot anvil about to crack. There was whining and tapping at the windows, but it was neither the winter wynd nor Marley's ghost: it was mosquito and bluebottle. It felt odd.

Her mother, Joy noticed, chose the bed in the corner and kept sitting on it, as if to keep this unforeseen Christmas from creeping up on her. She too was uneasy. Dad simply kept wondering how much the car would cost, and fingering the hotel's tariff card. Finally his wife took it out of his hand and whispered, 'Think of the caravan.' After that, he read the newspaper instead. Perhaps that was his way of shutting out the strangeness.

Once a week, a refrigerated van left Kendal with twenty turkeys for delivery to Forever Xmas. Each day two or three or four were set to roast in the extra-large ovens of Mrs Partridge's kitchen. She bought cranberry sauce by the crate from the cash-and-carry in Keswick, along with crackers and pudding and Paxo. For 364 days of the year, Colin and Ivy Partridge staged Christmas for anyone who, for whatever reason, omitted to celebrate it on December 25th.

Twice a week, a coach also brought parties of pensioners, friendly societies, women's clubs, British Legionnaires from the unfestive cities of Newcastle, Manchester, or Liverpool on outings to the fells and tarns of Wasthwaite to sing carols, eat turkey, and giggle at the folly of what they were doing. The day trippers gave themselves up to an afternoon of unreality, and left after tea-and-fruitcake.

But for those who stayed longer – two, maybe three nights – the game was played in earnest. Fathers who worked overseas, nurses and policemen on duty over Christmas, relations visiting from Australia – anyone cheated of a traditional British Christmas with their children – could look to Forever Xmas to supply the full gamut of festivities, from a blazing log fire to a visit from Father Christmas. Mrs Partridge's father filled that particular role, come rain, come snow, come heatwaves.

For the Shepherds, straying in on this 'unique tourist facility', it was a bizarre culture shock – like breaking into an asylum for the Christmasly insane. Ivy and Colin Partridge appeared to be the glummest people in all Cumbria: she with her hair rolled up round her head like an inflatable dinghy, he shiny with Brylcreem and over-ironing.

But the mechanic at the local garage said he had to send away for a spare part for the car. And it might take twenty-four hours to come.

That evening, when they went down to supper, there were four other tables occupied. Cliff Richard drizzled quietly out of speakers in all four corners of the room, and two of the turkey carcasses stood as centre-pieces to a buffet, with thick brown soup to start. All the windows were open, to encourage a through-draught, but since the sky outside was still a bright summery blue, the plush curtains had been drawn across to shut out the view of incandescent Cold Pike and to let the Christmas tree lights twinkle in the gloom.

At one table a huge muscular man with close-cropped hair barked loudly at a boy and a girl, like a boisterous dog wanting to be played with. 'Well then? Open it, open it!' A succession of shiny carrier bags were heaved across the table. The children responded – like shark fed on offal – with a feeding frenzy of eagerness, then played with large, noisy flashing vehicles and weapons on the table top, swerving between the plates, blasting each other across the pickle jars. Now and then, their mother mentioned table manners, but was ignored.

A party of Japanese teenage girls, dressed in expensive clothes, photographed each other in front of the Christmas tree, in front of the unlit Yule log, in front of the turkey carcasses, and raising their glasses in a toast to Christmas. Though the food was repugnant to them, they were observing the true customs of a foreign country, and they did it with the scrupulous, methodical thoroughness their friends would expect of them when they arrived home with their incomprehensible memories and two thousand photographs.

At another table, a father harangued his two daughters furiously, banging with the handle of his knife on the table and scowling and whispering loudly, while the children sat round-shouldered, eyelids half-closed against the onslaught of criticism. Only occasional snatches of the tirade reached as far as Joy. 'Look at you … way she dresses you … that woman … if I had any say … wouldn't be allowed …' His children ate in silence, their eyes drifting to the tree as at home they drifted to the refuge of a TV set.

Last of all, in the darkest corner of the room, a man and boy sat opposite each other, his hands spread over the boy's, their platefuls of food barely touched. They seemed to have nothing whatsoever to say to one another.

Joy's mother was feeling guilty. Her relief at *not* reaching Linstock and the caravan pricked like a goad. Guiltily, she kept going to the pay phone in the hall to call Gran and Grandpa and say how sorry she was they had been delayed. The line was busy. She tried every five minutes. She was also worried about the effect Forever Xmas was having on Mel.

'What do you mean? He's in heaven,' said Joy.

'Exactly,' said Mrs Shepherd watching the four year old croon to himself as he gazed at the Christmas tree. 'All these people having Christmas, and we're not.'

'Aren't we? How can you tell?' asked Joy. She had just then been trying to get to grips with the philosophy of the thing. Was it the date – 25th December – which constituted Christmas, or was it what people did by consensus on 25th December which made 25th December Christmas? That is to say, was 25th December still Christmas on uninhabited islands, even with no one to observe it? Or could August 12th just as well be Christmas if, by public accord, the world agreed to have it then? Was it all in the anticipation, perhaps? The result of people expecting it to happen? Had they, the Shepherds, jumped out on it and taken Christmas by surprise wearing its curlers and without a smile on its face? Or did the weather have something to do with it …?

At this point, Mel, suddenly remembering that socks were crucial to Christmas, pulled off his shoes and threw them across the table. Brown Windsor soup tipped, like slurry from a dredger, into Joy's lap, and a glass of orange juice went over too.

'You'd best go and get changed,' said her mother. 'Rinse it through before it stains.'

'I've finished anyway,' said Joy.

'You don't want this Christmas pud?' said her father reaching across.

'Children don't,' said Joy scornfully. Lately she had noticed how often her father needed telling such things. The knowledge did not seem to be inborn, as it was in mothers.

No, she thought, as she battled upstairs through a dozen spring-loaded fire-doors, the weather could have nothing to do with it. Australians always had this kind of weather at Christmas. So where was it, then, Christmas? Without knowing, Joy was in search of it now – behind the fire-doors, beyond earshot of 'Jingle Bells'. She opened the door of their bedroom …

… And found an elf crouching in the fire-grate with her hand up the chimney.

She was large for an elf, small for a teenager – a pinch-faced, dark-haired girl in white tights and a green sateen blouse rucked at the seams and creased at the elbows and shirt-tail. She wore a carrier bag over her hand so that the soot from the chimney did not dirty her sleeve. She wore ballet shoes and red face-painted cheeks which exaggerated the paleness of her skin and made her look feverish, embarrassed.

'What are you doing?' said Joy. 'I'm going to get my dad.'

'No! Wait! I was just …' The elf jumped up. She was about Joy's age, eleven or twelve, and painfully thin, with darting dark eyes. 'I was just doing you for wishes.'

Joy barred the door, arms folded, She had ambitions to be in the police. The elf had ambitions to get away, that much was plain. 'Doing us for what?' said Joy.

'You know? The forms? Your Christmas wish? Haven't you filled yours in yet?'

'What forms?'

'You know? Everybody gets one. Letter to Santa. Fill in the gaps. What you want. From Santa. Mam likes to know. Supposed to leave them in the grate. I collect them. Sometimes people shove them up the chimney. That's where I was …' she managed to combine a look of sleepiness with a desperate agitation – like an insomniac craving a good night's sleep. Joy flopped on to one of the beds. The elf sat down on another with a gesture of defeat. 'You're not supposed to see me,' she said. 'I'm not supposed to talk to the visitors.'

But she did.

Holly was the only daughter of Colin and Ivy Partridge; also their only elf. The firm of Forever Xmas was a family enterprise and did not earn sufficient to employ outside staff. So Holly came home from school to a perpetual round of elf-help: waiting at table, cleaning rooms, wrapping gifts, and playing with little children. People did not often bring children of Holly's age to Forever Xmas. The sudden and unexpected sight of Joy seemed to breach some dam inside her and out poured trade secrets.

'The lottery's made things easier,' said the elf, crossing her laddered white legs. 'Now most people wish to win the lottery. So they get lottery dice. Cheap. They used to put "the Premium Bonds" or the pools. Too expensive. Gift vouchers are ten pounds a go. We couldn't do it. Now it's lottery dice. 99p all up. The turkeys on the coaches are easiest: the old folk. Children want *so much*; write down masses of things. No end to it. The old folk, they either want peace in the world or to win the lottery.'

'What do they get if they ask for peace?' asked Joy, drawn into this grotto world of wish-fulfilment.

'A Marks and Spencer's voucher. Quite often they wish to get back together soon with Bill or Eric – a husband or something – someone who's dead. People are funny about wishing if they think nobody might read it.'

'What then? Do you kill them off or give them a wreath?'

'No. We bung them a bottle of Sanatogen – in case being run down is making them weepy. *I* wanted to do them pirate videos of *Stairway to Heaven* with David Niven, but Mam said old people don't have VCRs much … We do *try*, you know.' She said it defensively, resentfully, as if Joy had impugned her professionalism as an elf. And yet every strand of her fine, dishevelled hair dripped disillusionment. 'It's worse when the kids …' (she said it as if she were not one, had never been one) 'when the kids ask for things like that too. *Wish Mum and Dad would stop fighting* – things like that. That's a killer.' And suddenly, quite unexpectedly, big tears rolled down on to her red cheeks and skidded off in all directions across the greasy paint. Joy recoiled, her sandal buckle snagging the candlewick bedcover. For the first time that day, she wished she was in Linstock.

The elf blew her nose. 'They used to like Christmas – Mam and Dad. Their favourite time, it was. Some people say it just makes extra work and costs a lot. But Mam and Dad they loved it. Got married at Christmas. Had me … All those old films TV puts on at Christmas: Mam and Dad love all them. It came to them in a flash. Nowhere else does it. There had to be a place for it. "In business, all you need is a good idea," Dad said. Year-round Christmas. That was their good idea.'

'And now they hate it,' said Joy, meaning to be sympathetic.

Her voice startled the elf into an awareness that she had spoken out of turn. 'I didn't say that! Of course not! Mam'd kill me if I said that. I didn't say that. It's all right. It's fine.' With a look of guilty panic, Holly Partridge jumped up, straightened the rumpled bedcover and, picking up the waste-paper basket to empty, darted out of the room.

Back at the dinner table Mum and Dad had had a bottle of wine and were holding hands. Dad had had to put the business supplement of his *Telegraph* under the wet tablecloth to save the shine. Even though the shine was Formica. It left him nothing to do but talk to his wife. Mel was playing in the Adventure Corner – a plastic slide, a foam cushion, and three beanbags.

'I brought these down from the bedroom,' said Mum, suddenly and gleefully remembering. She brought the questionnaires out of her bag and held them at arm's length to read. *A LETTER TO SNATA* said the misprint on the back. 'Apparently we have to fill them in and leave them in the fire-grate for Father Christmas,' she read.

'Snata Claus is coming to town,' said Dad derisively.

Anne Shepherd was giggly after the wine and ignored him. She wrote that she hoped the car would take a week to mind.

Joy said, 'I'll think about it. I don't know what to put,' and she folded the sheet and pocketed it. 'But we're not doing Christmas. You said.' She resolved not to fill it in at all, not to be one of the stereotypes Holly Partridge had divided the human race into.

But when Mel came running over, Joy at once offered him a lap and to write down his wishes for him. She would never have dreamed of denting the Christmas magic for her little brother, of trying to extinguish the shine in Mel's eyes.

'I want a white Power Ranger and a Megazord and a Mr Muscle and a Car Breakers …' The shine turned to a gleam, a beady voracious hunger that made Mel curl and uncurl the fingers of both hands like a raptor stretching its claws.

Joy tried to quieten him – thought of the elf and wanted to silence and soothe him. 'Wouldn't you like to ask for something kind? What about all the little children who haven't got any toys or even enough to … Wouldn't you like to make a kind wish for th–'

She withered under Mel's glare. His top lip rucked into a snarl. 'No!' he said. 'I want a white Power Ranger and a Megazord and Mr Muscle …'

'Santa can't carry all that in this weather,' said Joy opening her knees so that her little brother slipped to the floor. 'He'd get heatstroke.'

'That's right,' said their mother gratefully. 'Things like that have to wait until December. What are you going to wish for, darling?' Tenderly she relinquished her husband's writing hand and found him a pen.

'A win on the lottery would do me nicely,' said Mr Shepherd, grinning round at them.

'*No!*' His daughter's ferocity startled him. '*No!*'

It startled Joy, too, to find she objected so much to her father's wish. But she did. She realized, with a pang of shame, that she was glaring at him, her mouth rucked into a snarl.

Mel began to grizzle and whine. Jack Shepherd screwed up his letter to Snata and pitched it into the open, unlit hearth saying, 'I tell you what: I wish this place were a thing of the past for all of us.' He pushed his face belligerently across the table at his disapproving children; wine always made him ratty in the end. 'I wish a plague on Father Christmas and on this place. I can't wait to get back to work and some peace and civility.'

'And I want –' said Mel from under the table.

'*Oh, shut up, Mel!*' said everyone.

Read, Think and Write

1. Where were the Shepherd family travelling to and how were they feeling about the journey?

2. What was the result of the 'blizzard of white' that flurried past the car window?

3. After the Shepherds abandoned their car, what was the 'slab of metal and glass' that 'hurtled down on them' and why was it viewed as both a danger and a hopeful sign?

4. What impression of the 'large white building' do the Shepherd family have as they approach the house and stand waiting for the door to open?

5. Why are they shocked and surprised when the door opens?

6. 'Is the Christmas bit obligatory?' What does this mean and how does Mrs Partridge react to the question?

7. Make a list of all the symbols of Christmas throughout the text, e.g. Shepherd, donkey, miniature pine trees.

8. Who owns Forever X? Look for descriptions in the text to show how the owners organise and run the place.

9. Find examples in the text to show the reactions of each of the Shepherd family to their stay at Forever X. For example, Mel was excited as he ran 'from snow-caked window to tinselled toilet cistern'.

10. Write a summary of how the occupants of the four other tables at suppertime are feeling about their stay at Forever X.

11. ' "We do try you know." She said it defensively, resentfully, as if Joy had impugned her professionalism as an elf.' What is Holly's job and why is she so disillusioned?

12. How does the conversation with Holly affect Joy's behaviour later? Is Joy right to question stereotypes? Why does she get so upset?

Read and Analyse

1. 'An octopus of paper-chains hung between the centre lampshade and the picture rails.'
   '… she with her hair rolled up round her head like an inflatable dinghy, …'

   The author uses many descriptive images throughout this opening. Study the text carefully and write down ten examples of the use of simile and metaphor.

2. 'And yet every strand of her fine, dishevelled hair dripped disillusionment.'

   This sentence describes Holly Partridge. Write a descriptive sentence for each of her parents and each of the Shepherd family, using alliteration.

3. Two more guests arrive at Forever X. Who are they? What circumstances have brought them to the house? Write a descriptive passage about them and their arrival. Start your writing with one of the Partridges opening the door and being as surprised as the Shepherds were on seeing 'Father Christmas'.

Hint
Use simile, metaphor and alliteration to create unusual and interesting images in your writing.

Read, Discuss and Act

1. 'I wish a plague on Father Christmas and on this place.' Mr Shepherd's comment gives a sense of foreboding to the opening of the story. Do you dread Christmas or enjoy it? Share and discuss Christmas experiences.

2. Do you think a themed hotel like Forever X is a good idea? Look back at your answer to question 10 about the occupants of the other four tables and discuss people's motivation for attending such a place. What other themes might work?

3. Develop the suppertime scene at Forever X. Choose one of the tables described in the text and role-play the conversation that might take place between the characters. (The Japanese can just speak English!)

Abomination

by Robert Swindells

The author uses the point of view of two characters to tell this story. Martha and Scott are the narrators and it is through them that the plot unfolds. Martha and her family have a secret …

2. Scott

I think it's going to be all right, Southcott Middle. I'm in Mr Wheelwright's class. He's OK. Looks like Rolf Harris but likes computers and supports Man United so can't be all bad. The kids're OK too, apart from a snob or two and a few veg, but you always get those. There's a terrific playing-field, and at lunchtime after your meal you can play on the computers in the library. You've got to be quick, mind – there're only ten computers and it's first come first served, but that's fair. A great white shark can't wreck a dinner quicker than me.

Oh, I nearly forgot. There's this really weird girl, Martha Dewhurst. The kids laughed yesterday because Wheelwright put me on her table. I didn't know why they were laughing till morning break, when this guy called Simon came up to me and said, 'Keep your head away from Raggedy-Ann's if you don't want nits.' That's her nickname – Raggedy-Ann. I don't think she has nits, but there's like a gap between her and everybody else on our table, and nobody'll lend her their rubber. She has these funny clothes. I mean, they're *uniform* – maroon sweater, grey skirt – but they're not like everyone else's. I think her mum must've made them. Or her gran.

There's this game after school, Chase Raggedy-Ann. Some kid'll start chanting – *chase Raggedy-Ann, chase Raggedy-Ann* – like that. A few others join in, and when there's about ten they set off after her. I didn't go yesterday – felt a bit sorry for her if you must know – but I did today because Simon started it and he's my friend. She looks really funny, running.

She's got these very thin, long legs that splay out sort of sideways as she runs, and her arms are all over the place too. I doubt she'll ever run for England. The kids don't try to catch her – it'd be over straight away if they did – so they hang back, running about fifty metres behind her, chanting *Raggedy-Ann, Raggedy Ann, we'll all scrag you if we can.* She doesn't seem to know they're not trying to catch her. You can tell she's going full belt. She lives up this very steep slope called Taylor Hill. Her house is near the top, and she's near collapsing by the time she reaches the gate. We pull up and watch her stagger up the path like a shot bandit, then we walk back down the hill, laughing and joking and taking turns with a ciggy.

I reckon I'll be fine at my new school.

3. Martha

My favourite time is after dinner when I have the place to myself. Father's an agent for an insurance company. He does his round at night because that's when people are in, and Mother works the evening shift at a soft toy factory.

I have the washing-up to do and Abomination's mess to see to, but after that I'm free till ten, except in winter when it's nine thirty. We don't have TV. I sometimes listen to Radio One, but I've got to remember not to leave the set tuned to that station when I switch off, because the Righteous believe the devil reaches young people through pop music. The Righteous is our church. One night last year I forgot, and when Father switched on for the morning news he got Madonna and I got the rod. It's a cane really, but Father calls it the rod. His favourite text is *Train up a child in the way he should go: and when he is old, he will not depart from it.* Notice it says *he*, not *she*. It's not about girls, but Father seems not to have spotted that and I daren't point it out.

They're administered really carefully by the way, my beatings. Oh, yes. Wouldn't do for some busybody to spot the marks on me. They're always on my bum, so they're covered in PE and even when I swim. I could show somebody of course, but then Father would get into trouble and I wouldn't want to be responsible for that. He thinks he's doing the best thing, you see: that it's for my own good.

Anyway, after twirling round the kitchen to a few of the devil's tunes, I usually go up to my room and look at Mary's postcards. Mary's my big sister. Father sent her away when I was six. She's grown up and has a really interesting life if the cards are anything to go by. They're from all over: London, Liverpool, Birmingham. There's even one from Amsterdam. Some are addressed to Mother and Father and some are to me. I'm not supposed to have any of them. Father tears them up unread and throws them in the bin, but I rescue them and stick them back together with sellotape. I've been doing this since I was six. I couldn't read then, but I knew who they were from and the pictures were nice. I've got thirty-one now, in a shoe-box under the floor, with my Blur poster, four *Point Horror* books and a few other things my parents wouldn't like.

Mother says we're special because we're Righteous, but that doesn't make me feel better. I'd rather not be special if it means having to hide things.

If I can't have friends round.

If I can't have friends.

4. Scott

Saturday morning I'd arranged to meet Simon down town so he could show me round, but I nearly didn't get to keep the appointment. We lived near Birmingham before, and my folks never let me go into the city by myself. Twelve's too young they'd say, though some of my friends did it every weekend. When I mentioned it Friday night, there was a row. You'd no business making arrangements like that without asking, they said. We don't know this boy. This Simon. You better phone him and say you won't be there.

I talked 'em round, but only because I didn't have Simon's number. Dad said to look it up in the book, but I pretended I didn't know his surname. I do of course – it's Pritchard – but he wasn't to know that. In the end him and Mum decided that because Scratchley's a small place it would probably be OK. I was really chuffed – like they'd finally noticed I'm not a little kid any more. I felt like dancing round the room, thumping the air and going *Yes!*, but I didn't. I acted dead cool.

Lying in bed that night I started thinking about Martha. Don't ask me why. I'd helped chase her home Wednesday and Thursday, but I hadn't joined in today and neither had Simon. We'd been too busy making our arrangements. Others had gone after her though. I don't think she ever gets to just walk home like everybody else. I feel sorry for her in a way but she makes me angry too. I know that sounds strange, but it's a fact. It irritates me the way she puts up with everything. I mean, if she told someone – Mr Wheelwright or one of the other teachers – they'd *do* something, wouldn't they? They'd put a stop to it, or try to. At the very least there'd by an Assembly about bullying. And in class, she pretends not to notice the space round her chair, or that nobody speaks to her. She doesn't ask to borrow anything or try to start a conversation. She sits with her eyes down, concentrating on her work, and if Wheelwright asks her a question she ignores the sniggers and answers quietly, and it's usually the right answer. It's as if nothing can push her over the edge. She's like some helpless little animal. Never cries.

Anyway I lay a long time thinking about her and had a restless night, so that when I met Simon in the shopping centre it felt more like ten at night than ten in the morning. I wondered what he'd say if I told him I was being bugged by Raggedy-Ann. Not that I would. When you've only one friend, you want to keep him.

5. Martha

Scott lent me his ruler today. I'd used mine at home and forgotten to put it back in my bag. I didn't ask him. He saw me rummaging and said, 'Lost something?' 'Yes,' I whispered. 'My ruler.' I expected him to snigger and say tough or something like that, but he didn't. He just pushed his ruler towards me. I looked up to see if he meant to snatch it away when I went to pick it up, but he was writing. I underlined my heading and slid the ruler back across the table. 'Thanks.' ''S'OK.' He didn't look up. Tracy Stamper snorted. 'I'd burn that now if I were you. It's contaminated.' Scott ignored her.

I know what you're thinking. You're thinking, *So what? Why's she banging on about someone lending her their ruler?* Well, I know it's no big deal to you. Kids borrow one another's stuff all the time, but not me. Nobody ever lent me anything till today, or borrowed anything of mine. So although it only happened that one time, and though Scott didn't speak or even look at me again, it mattered. It made my day. I didn't even mind when they chased me home In fact I was glad, because Scott wasn't with them. If you've never been ignored it'll just sound daft to you.

What I'd like most of all is somebody to talk to. About my life. About how things are at home. See – I *know* why the kids hate me. I know I seem weird to them, but it's not me. It's not. Inside I'm just like them. I like pop music and TV and clothes but I can't have them. They're forbidden. I'd like to have a party, invite everybody on my table, but I can't even bring a friend home. I mean, there are kids at church. Righteous kids. They see one another, play together, but not me. I can't bring anybody to the house in case they find out about Abomination. I can go to *their* homes – I used to – but I never invited them back so they stopped bothering with me and you can't blame them, but if there was just one person who understood, one person who *knew*, I think I could stand it.

So. It's seven o'clock, my parents are out and I'm lying on my bed constructing a fantasy. I do this a lot. It's my way of escaping for a while. This particular fantasy is different from most because it's based on fact – the fact that Scott lent me his ruler. In my fantasy, I go up to him at break and thank him, and we get talking and it turns out he fancies me. Wants to take me out. We go to a live Blur concert. My parents think I'm at Bible class. From then on we're inseparable, Scott and me. One day he finds Gordon Linfoot giving me an Indian burn behind the bike sheds and beats him up. Another time it's a maths exam and he's completely stuck and I slip him all the answers on a bit of paper. We come joint top, and to celebrate we take a train to London, staying in a posh hotel and buying all the latest fashions on Oxford Street. Mother and Father know nothing about it – they're in comas after a car crash.

Amazing what it can lead to, borrowing someone's ruler.

Read, Think and Write

If a writer is telling a story from the point of view of a character, then it can be very important to the plot that the reader understands how the character feels and experiences the other characters they interact with and the situation around them.

1. 'I think it's going to be all right, Southcott Middle.' Write down some examples from the text to show how Scott feels about school.

2. 'And in class, she pretends not to notice the space round her chair, or that nobody speaks to her.' Write down examples from the text which show how Martha experiences school, seen from Scott's point of view.

3. 'I wondered what he'd say if I told him I was being bugged by Raggedy-Ann.' What effect has Martha on Scott? Find evidence in the text to show how he reacts to Martha and what he thinks about her.

4. 'I expected him to snigger and say tough or something like that, but he didn't.' What effect has Scott on Martha? Find evidence in the text to show how she reacts to Scott and what she thinks about him.

5. 'My favourite time is after dinner when I have the place to myself.' Gather evidence from the text to show what Martha's home life is like.

6. 'Saturday morning I'd arranged to meet Simon down town so he could show me round …' Gather evidence from the text to show what life is like for Scott out of school hours.

7. In your own words, write a comparison between the home life of Scott and Martha. How are their experiences of friends and family different?

8. Write a character study of either Scott or Martha.

Read and Analyse

1. The author has written in a style that tries to capture the thoughts of two characters. He uses punctuation which helps give the 'talking in the mind' effect. Dashes are used to show an aside or an afterthought. Look through the text and write down some examples of the use of dashes.

> **Example**
> I didn't go yesterday – felt a bit sorry for her if you must know – but I did today because Simon started it and he's my friend.

Write five sentences of your own, using dashes to show an aside or an afterthought.

2. When we speak we usually shorten words. Look through the text again to see how often the author has used contractions to give a more conversational tone to the writing. Find and write down ten examples.

> **Example**
> *there're* – there are   *kid'll* – kid will

Read, Discuss and Act

1. Martha is obviously a victim of bullying. Consider and discuss these questions.
   What makes someone bully others?
   Are certain types of people more likely to be victims?
   Are there different kinds of bullying?
   Do girls bully people differently from boys?
   Is it just children who bully others?
   What other contexts might bullying occur in? Think back to Martha's home life. Is her father a bully?

2. Martha has to look after 'Abomination'. Who or what do you think this is? Keeping a secret may involve trusting someone. Are there times when it may be difficult or wrong to keep a secret?

3. In pairs, role-play a conversation between Scott and Martha where they tell each other about their experiences of and feelings about school and their home life. Develop the characters further by having them discuss and share their interests and hopes for the future.

Mrs Midas

by Carol Ann Duffy

Uncle Edward's Affliction

by Vernon Scannell

The Singing Foot

by Spike Milligan

Carol Ann Duffy's poem develops a character to give a different interpretation of the story of King Midas. In his desire for everything he touches to be turned to gold, Midas wishes upon himself an affliction, the consequences of which are shown through the feelings and observations of Mrs Midas. Vernon Scannell's poem considers a more realistic affliction and its effect upon the sufferer, whereas the character in Spike Milligan's short story has to cope with a rather unusual physical sensation!

Mrs Midas

It was late September. I'd just poured a glass of wine, begun
to unwind, while the vegetables cooked. The kitchen
filled with the smell of itself, relaxed, its steamy breath
gently blanching the windows. So I opened one,
then with my fingers wiped the other's glass like a brow.
He was standing under the pear-tree snapping a twig.

Now the garden was long and the visibility poor, the way
the dark of the ground seems to drink the light of the sky,
but that twig in his hand was gold. And then he plucked
a pear from a branch, we grew Fondante d'Automne,
and it sat in his palm like a light-bulb. On.
I thought to myself, Is he putting fairy lights in the tree?

He came into the house. The doorknobs gleamed.
He drew the blinds. You know the mind; I thought of
the Field of the Cloth of Gold and of Miss Macready.
He sat in that chair like a king on a burnished throne.
The look on his face was strange, wild, vain; I said,
What in the name of God is going on? He started to laugh.

I served up the meal. For starters, corn on the cob.
Within seconds he was spitting out the teeth of the rich.
He toyed with his spoon, then mine, then with the knives, the forks.
He asked where was the wine. I poured with a shaking hand,
a fragrant bone-dry white from Italy, then watched
as he picked up the glass, goblet, golden chalice, drank.

It was then that I started to scream. He sank to his knees.
After we'd both calmed down, I finished the wine
on my own, hearing him out. I made him sit
on the other side of the room and keep his hands to himself.
I locked the cat in the cellar. I moved the phone.
The toilet I didn't mind. I couldn't believe my ears:

how he'd had a wish. Look, we all have wishes; granted.
But who has wishes granted? Him. Do you know about gold?
It feeds no one; aurum, soft, untarnishable; slakes
no thirst. He tried to light a cigarette; I gazed, entranced,
as the blue flame played on its luteous stem. At least,
I said, you'll be able to give up smoking for good.`

Separate beds. In fact, I put a chair against my door,
near petrified. He was below, turning the spare room
into the tomb of Tutankhamen. You see, we were passionate then,
in those halcyon days; unwrapping each other, rapidly,
like presents, fast food. But now I feared his honeyed embrace,
the kiss that would turn my lips to a work of art.

And who, when it comes to the crunch, can live
with a heart of gold? That night, I dreamt I bore
his child, its perfect ore limbs, its little tongue
like a precious latch, its amber eyes
holding their pupils like flies. My dream-milk
burned in my breasts. I woke to the streaming sun.

So he had to move out. We'd a caravan
in the wilds, in a glade of its own. I drove him up
under cover of dark. He sat in the back.
And then I came home, the woman who married the fool
who wished for gold. At first I visited, odd times,
parking the car a good way off, then walking.

You knew you were getting close. Golden trout
on the grass. One day, a hare hung from a larch,
a beautiful lemon mistake. And then his footprints,
glistening next to the river's path. He was thin,
delirious; hearing, he said, the music of Pan
from the woods. Listen. That was the last straw.

What gets me now is not the idiocy or greed
but lack of thought for me. Pure selfishness. I sold
the contents of the house and came down here.
I think of him in certain lights, dawn, late afternoon,
and once a bowl of apples stopped me dead. I miss most,
even now, his hands, his warm hands on my skin, his touch.

Uncle Edward's Affliction

Uncle Edward was colour-blind;
We grew accustomed to the fact.
When he asked someone to hand him
The green book from the window-seat
And we observed its bright red cover
Either apathy or tact
Stifled comment. We passed it over.
Much later, I began to wonder
What a curious world he wandered in,
Down streets where pea-green pillar boxes
Grinned at a fire-engine as green;
How Uncle Edward's sky at dawn
And sunset flooded marshy green.
Did he ken John Peel with his coat so green
And Robin Hood in Lincoln red?
On country walks avoid being stung
By nettles hot as a witch's tongue?
What meals he savoured with his eyes:
Green strawberries and fresh red peas,
Green beef and greener burgundy.
All unscientific, so it seems:
His world was not at all like that,
So those who claim to know have said.
Yet, I believe, in war-smashed France
He must have crawled from neutral mud
To lie in pastures dark and red
And seen, appalled, on every blade
The rain of innocent green blood.

The Singing Foot

Woy Woy, Australia.
September 1967.

I have an Uncle. His name is Herbert Jam. He was 52. He worked in a laundry. One Christmas Eve he was homeward bound on a crowded bus when he heard what he thought was the sound of music coming from inside his boot; indeed, what was to make him famous had happened, his right foot had commenced to sing. Poor Mr. Jam tried to control the volume of sound by tightening his boot lace; it only succeeded in making the voice go from a deep baritone to a strangled tenor. At the next stop Mr. Jam had to get off. He walked home to the sound of his right foot singing 'God rest you merry gentlemen'. Fortunately, Mr. Jam knew the words and mimed them whenever people passed by. It was all very, very embarrassing. For three days he stayed off work. His favourite T.V. programmes were ruined by unexpected bursts of song from the foot. He did manage to deaden it by watching with his foot in a bucket of sand, but, alas, from this practice he contracted a rare foot rot normally only caught by Arabs and camels. Worse was to come. The foot started singing at night. At three in the morning he was awakened with selections from 'The Gondoliers', 'Drake is going West' and 'A Whiter Shade of Pale'. He tried Mrs. Helen Furg, a lady who was known to have exorcised Poltergeists and Evil Spirits. She tied a sprig of witchhazel round his ankle, intoned druidic prayers and burnt all his socks in the bath, but it wasn't long before the strains of 'The Desert Song' came lilting up his trouser leg again. On the recommendation of his doctor he visited the great Harley Street right-foot specialist, Sir Ralph Fees.

" Come in, sit down," said the great man. "Now what appears to be our trouble?"

"It's my right foot."

"Of course it is," said cheery Sir Ralph, "and" he went on, "what appears to be the trouble with our right foot?"

"It sings."

Sir Ralph paused (but still went on charging). "You say your foot sings?"

"Yes, it's a light baritone," said wretched Jam.

Sir Ralph started to write. "I want you to go and see this Psychiatrist" he said – at which very moment Uncle Herbert's foot burst into song! "Just a minute" said Sir Ralph. "I'll get my hat and come with you."

The medical world and Harley Street were baffled. For the time he had to make do with a surgical sound-proof boot and a pair of wax ear-plugs. Occasionally, he would take off his boot give the lads at the Pub a song, but Mr. Jam was far from happy. Then came the beginning of the end. E.M.I. gave him a £500,000,000 contract for his foot to make records. A special group was formed, called 'The Grave'; the billing was 'Mr. Jam with One Foot in the Grave'. He was the news sensation of the year! But, it became clear that it was the right foot that got the fame, not Mr. Jam. E.M.I. opened a bank account for the right foot. While his poor left foot wore an old boot, his right foot wore expensive purple alligator shoes from Carnaby Street which cost £50 a toe. At parties he was ceaselessly taking off his shoe to sign autographs! Mr. Jam was just an embarrassment to his right foot! One night in a fit of jealousy Mr. Jam shot his foot through the instep. It never sang again! Mr. Jam returned to the obscurity of his job in the laundry. He was 52, happy, only now he walked with a slight limp.

Read, Think and Write

1. Where was Midas and what was he doing at the beginning of the poem by Carol Ann Duffy?

2. Can you find evidence in the poem to show that at first Mrs Midas did not understand what was happening?

3. What were her first reactions after she heard what had happened to her husband?

4. What did Mrs Midas fear?

5. Where did Mrs Midas take her husband?

6. Make a list of phrases the poet uses to describe the changes Midas makes.

> **Example**
> *pear* — 'like a light bulb. On.'
> *corn on the cob* — 'he was spitting out the teeth of the rich'

7. What images does the poet use to personify the kitchen?

8. Why is the end of the poem ironic? Are there any other examples of irony in the poem?

9. What does Vernon Scannell mean by 'Either apathy or tact stifled comment.'?

10. What sort of view of Uncle Edward does the poet give? What effect does the ending of the poem have on this view?

11. What problems did the 'singing foot' create for Herbert Jam?

12. Rewrite *either* the poem 'Mrs Midas' *or* the short story 'The Singing Foot' as a tabloid newspaper article. Give your article a suitably sensational headline, such as 'Going for Gold' or 'The Defeat of a Bootiful Voice'.

Read and Analyse

1. Use a dictionary and a thesaurus to investigate the word 'colour'.

   What suffixes can you add to it?

   Hint
   Think about word class (noun, verb, etc.).

   Example
   colourful

   How might the suffixes alter word class?

   Find synonyms. Use 'colour' words in sentences to show their meaning.

2. Use a thesaurus to find synonyms for the noun 'greed' and the adjective 'greedy'. Write some sentences using these words.

3. Using the conventions for speech, write down the conversation that you imagine took place between Mrs Midas and her husband as they had their meal. You could begin:

   'What in the name of God is going on?' she asked.
   'Nothing. Don't worry,' he said laughing. 'What's for dinner?'

Read, Discuss and Act

1. What upsets Mrs Midas most about her husband's actions? Is she also being selfish or are there times when we have to think of ourselves first?

2. What does being greedy mean? Are there different kinds of greed?

   In groups, act out a short scene to demonstrate a form of greed.

3. In groups, construct and role-play scenes from a documentary programme entitled 'Strange Afflictions'. Mrs Midas could be one of the interviewees. Who else might be interviewed?

Housekeeping

by Marilynn Robinson

Ruth and Lucille are sisters. While they are still very young, their mother leaves them with their grandmother and then, despite some difficulty in her attempts at suicide, finally succeeds by driving her little car over a cliff into the sea. The girls grow up under the care of their grandmother. When she dies, her sisters-in-law, Lily and Nona Foster, arrange for the girls' aunt to come to the grandmother's house in the hope that she will look after the girls.

In the following extract, Sylvie, one of the central characters in the book, is introduced into the lives of Ruth and Lucille.

I have often wondered what it seemed like to Sylvie to come back to that house, which would have changed since she left it, shifted and settled. I imagine her with her grips in her bare hands, walking down the middle of the road, which was narrowed by the banks of plowed snow on either side, and narrowed more by the slushy pools that were forming at the foot of each bank. Sylvie always walked with her head down, to one side, with an abstracted and considering expression, as if someone were speaking to her in a soft voice. But she would have glanced up sometimes at the snow, which was the color of heavy clouds, and the sky, which was the color of melting snow, and all the slick black planks and sticks and stumps that erupted as the snow sank away.

How must it have seemed to step into the narrow hallway which still kept (as it seemed to me) a trace of the rude odor that the funeral flowers had begun to make before Nona could bring herself to throw them away. Her hands and feet must have ached from the warmth. I remember how red and twisted her hands looked, lying in the lap of her green dress, and how she pressed her arms to her sides. I remember that, as she sat there in a wooden chair in the white kitchen, smoothing her borrowed-looking dress and working her feet out of her loafers, sustaining all our stares with the placid modesty of a virgin who has conceived, her happiness was palpable.

The day after Sylvie arrived, Lucille and I woke up early. It was our custom to prowl the dawn of any significant day. Ordinarily the house would belong to us for an hour or more, but that morning we found Sylvie sitting in the kitchen by the stove, with her coat on, eating oyster crackers from a small cellophane bag. She blinked at us, smiling. "It was nice with the light off," she suggested, and Lucille and I collided in our haste to pull the chain. Sylvie's coat made us think she might be leaving, and we were ready to perform great feats of docility to keep her. "Isn't that nicer?" In fact, the wind was badgering the house, throwing frozen rain against the windows. We sat down on the rug by her feet and watched her. She handed us each an oyster cracker. "I can hardly believe I'm here," she said finally. "I was on the train for eleven hours. There's so much snow in the mountains. We just crept along, for hours and hours and hours." It was clear from her voice that the trip had been pleasant. "Have you ever been on a train?" We had not. "They have heavy white tablecloths in the dining car, and little silver vases bolted to the window frame, and you get your own little silver pot of hot syrup. I like to travel by train," Sylvie said. "Especially in the passenger cars. I'll take you with me sometime."

"Take us where?" Lucille asked.

Sylvie shrugged. "Somewhere. Wherever. Where do you want to go?"

I saw the three of us posed in all the open doors of an endless train of freight cars – innumerable, rapid, identical images that produced a flickering illusion of both movement and stasis, as the pictures in a kinetoscope do. The hot and dangerous winds of our passing tattered the Queen Anne's lace, and yet, for all the noise and clatter and headlong speed, we flickered there at the foot of the garden while the train roared on and on. "Spokane," I said.

"Oh, somewhere better than that. Farther away. Maybe Seattle." There was a silence. "But that's where you used to live."

"With our mother," Lucille said.

"Yes." Sylvie had folded the empty cellophane wrapper in quarters and she was creasing the folds between finger and thumb.

"Would you tell us about her?" Lucille asked. The question was abrupt, and the tone of it was coaxing, because adults did not wish to speak to us about our mother. Our grandmother never spoke of any of her daughters, and when they were mentioned to her, she winced with irritation. We were accustomed to this, but not to the sharp embarrassment with which Lily and Nona and all my grandmother's friends reacted to our mother's very name. We had planned to try Sylvie, but perhaps because Sylvie had her coat on and appeared so very transient, Lucille did not wait till we knew her better, as we had agreed to do.

"Oh, she was nice," Sylvie said. "She was pretty."

"But what was she *like*?"

"She was good in school."

Lucille sighed.

"It's hard to describe someone you know so well. She was very quiet. She played the piano. She collected stamps." Sylvie seemed to be reflecting. "I've never known anyone so fond of cats. She was always bringing them home."

Lucille shifted her legs and adjusted the thick flannel skirt of her nightgown around them.

"I didn't see much of her after she was married," Sylvie explained.

"Then tell us about her wedding," Lucille said.

"Oh, that was very small. She wore a sundress made of eyelet lace, and a straw hat, and she had a bouquet of daisies. It was just to please Mother. They'd already been married by a justice of the peace somewhere in Nevada."

"Why Nevada?"

"Well, your father was from Nevada."

"What was he like?"

Sylvie shrugged. "He was tall. Not bad-looking. Awfully quiet, though, I think he was shy."

"What kind of work did he do?"

"He traveled. I think he sold some sort of farming equipment. Tools, maybe. I never even saw him except for that one day. Do you know where he is now?"

"Nope," I said. Lucille and I were remembering a day when Bernice had brought our mother a thick letter. "Reginald Stone," she had said, tapping the return address with a lavender claw. Helen gave her a cup of coffee and sat at the table picking idly at a loose corner of the postage stamp while Bernice whispered a scandalous tale of marital fracture and reconciliation involving a cocktail waitress Bernice knew very well. Apparently concluding at last that the letter would never be opened while she was there, Bernice finally left, and when she was gone Helen tore the envelope into fourths and dropped them in the trash. Glancing into our faces as if she suddenly remembered we were there, anticipating our questions, she said, "It's best," and that was all we knew of our father.

I could conjure her face as it was then, startled by the sudden awareness of our watching. At the time I think I felt only curiosity, though I suppose I remember that glance because she looked at me for signs of more than curiosity. And, in fact, I recall the moment now with some astonishment – there was neither doubt nor passion in her destruction of the letter, neither hesitation nor haste – and with frustration – there was only that letter and never another one, and nothing else from him or about him at all – and with anger – he was presumably our father, and might wish to know what had become of us, and even to intervene. It occurs to me sometimes that as I grow older I am increasingly able to present to her gaze the face she seemed to expect. But of course she was looking into a face I do not remember – no more like mine than Sylvie's is like hers. Less like, perhaps, because, as I watched Sylvie, she reminded me of my mother more and more. There was such similarity,

in fact, in the structure of cheek and chin, and the texture of hair, that Sylvie began to blur the memory of my mother, and then to displace it. Soon it was Sylvie who would look up startled, regarding me from a vantage of memory in which she had no place. And it was increasingly to this remembered Sylvie that I presented my look of conscious injury, knowing as I did so that Sylvie could know nothing of that letter.

What did Sylvie see when she thought of my mother? A girl with braided hair, a girl with freckled arms, who liked to lie on the rug in the lamplight, flat on her belly with her heels in the air and her chin on her two fists, reading Kipling. Did she tell lies? Could she keep secrets? Did she tickle, or slap, or pinch, or punch, or grimace? If someone had asked me about Lucille I would remember her with her mass of soft, fine, tangly hair concealing ears that cupped a bit and grew painfully cold if she did not cover them. I would remember that her front teeth, the permanent ones, came in, first one and much later the other, immense and raggedly serrated, and that she was fastidious about washing her hands. I would remember that when irked she bit her lip, when shy she scratched her knee, that she smelled dully clean, like chalk, or like a sun-warmed cat.

I do not think Sylvie was merely reticent. It is, as she said, difficult to describe someone, since memories are by their nature fragmented, isolated, and arbitrary as glimpses one has at night through lighted windows. …

"What would you like for breakfast?" Sylvie asked.

"Cornflakes."

She made cocoa and we ate and watched the day come. It had been a cold night that froze the slush and hardened the heaps of dirty, desiccated snow by the sides of the road.

"I'm going to take a little walk around town," Sylvie said. "Before the roads all turn to mud again. I'll be back soon." She buttoned her coat and stepped out into the porch. We heard the screen door slam. "She should have borrowed a scarf," I said. "She isn't coming back," Lucille replied. We ran upstairs and put on our jeans, stuffing the skirts of our nightgowns into them. We pulled our boots on over our bedroom slippers and grabbed our coats and ran outside, but she was gone already. If she was leaving, she would go into town, to the station. If she was not leaving, she would probably go to town anyway, unless she went to the lake. Since she was bareheaded, and had neither gloves nor boots, the shore would be miserably difficult and cold. We walked toward Main Street as fast as we could over the frozen slush and the frozen ruts and shards of ice. "I bet Lily and Nona told her to leave," I said. Lucille shook her head. Her face was flushed and her cheeks were wet. "It'll be all right," I said. She wiped her face roughly with her sleeve.

"I know it'll be all right, but it makes me mad."

We turned the corner and saw Sylvie in the road ahead of us, chucking chunks of ice at four or five dogs. She would pick up a bit of ice and toss it from hand to hand, walking backward, while the dogs followed after her and circled behind her, yapping. We saw her pelt one squat mongrel in the ribs, and all the dogs scattered. She sucked her fingers and blew into her cupped hands, and then picked up another piece of ice just as the dogs came back and began yapping and circling again. Her manner was insouciant and her aim was deft. She did not notice us standing at a distance watching her. We stood where we were until the last of the dogs turned and trotted back to its porch, and then we followed her at a distance of two blocks into downtown Fingerbone. She walked slowly past the drugstore and the dime store and the dry-goods store, stopping to look into each of the windows. Then she walked directly to the railroad station and went inside. Lucille and I walked down to the station. We could see her standing by the stove, with her arms folded, studying the chalked list of arrivals and departures. Lucille said, "I'm going to tell her she forgot her bags." I had not thought of that. When Sylvie saw us coming in she smiled with surprise. "You left your stuff at our house," Lucille said.

"Oh, I just came in here to get warm. Nothing else is open. It's early, you know. I forgot how early the sun rises these days." She rubbed her hands together in the warmth of the stove. "It still *feels* like winter, doesn't it?"

"Why don't you wear gloves?" Lucille asked.

"I left them on the train."

"Why don't you wear boots?"

Sylvie smiled. "I suppose I should."

"You also need a hat. You should use hand lotion."

Sylvie put her hands in her pockets. "I think I should stay for a while," she said. "The aunts are too old. I think it's best for now, at least."

Lucille nodded.

"We'll get some pie when the café opens. And then you can help me choose a scarf, and maybe some gloves." She groped in her pockets and brought out a little ball of paper money and some change. She looked at the money doubtfully and did not count it. "We'll see."

"We have hand lotion at home," Lucille replied.

At nine o'clock we followed Sylvie to the five-and-ten, where she bought a plaid scarf and gray gloves. It took her some time to choose them, and some time to explain who she was to the woman at the cash register, who, though Sylvie thought she looked familiar, was new in town and knew nothing of our family. When we came back into the street the sun was shining warmly. There was a bright flow of water in the gutters. When we came to the end of the sidewalk, there was no way for Sylvie to walk without now and then stepping over her shoes in water of one sort or another. This difficulty seemed to absorb her but not to disturb her.

"That woman reminded me of someone, but I can't think who," Sylvie said.

"Do you still have friends here?" Lucille asked.

Sylvie laughed. "Well, the fact is, I never did have many friends here. We kept to ourselves. We knew who everyone *was*, that's all. And now I've been away – sixteen years."

"But you came back sometimes," Lucille said.

"No."

"Where were you married?" Lucille asked.

"Here."

"Then that's once."

"Once," Sylvie said.

Lucille squashed a lump of slush with her boot, and I slapped her because some of it flew against my leg.

We went up the walk to our porch. Lily and Nona were in the kitchen, rosy with warmth and perturbation.

"Here you are!" Lily said.

"What a day to go walking!"

Sylvie had pried off her sodden loafers in the porch, and we had pulled off our coats and boots. The aunts clucked their tongues when they saw us in our jeans and slippers, and still in our nightgowns with our hair uncombed. "Ah!" they said. "What is this?"

Lucille said, "Ruthie and I woke up early this morning, and we decided to go outside to see the sun come up. We went clear downtown. Sylvie was worried, so she came out looking for us."

"Oh, I'm surprised at you girls," Nona said.

"Such a thoughtless thing to do."

"I hope Sylvie gave you a good talking-to."

"Poor Sylvie!"

"If we'd been here by ourselves, we'd have died of worry."

"We *would* have."

"The roads are so treacherous. What would we have done?"

They brought Sylvie a cup of coffee and a pan of hot water for her feet, clucking and commiserating and patting her hands and her hair.

"You have to be young to deal with children!"

"That's a fact."

"We'd have had to get the sheriff."

"It might have taught them a lesson."

The aunts hurried away to finish packing. Lucille opened the newspaper to the crossword puzzle, and found a pencil in a drawer and sat down across the table from Sylvie.

"The element represented by the symbol Fe," she said.

Sylvie answered, "Iron."

"Wouldn't it start with F?"

"It's iron," Sylvie said. "They try to trick you."

That evening Lily and Nona were taken by a friend of my grandmother's back to Spokane and we and the house were Sylvie's.

Read, Think and Write

1. Which character has the writer made the narrator of the story?

2. What is the first impression of Sylvie as she approaches and enters the house?

3. What do the girls learn about Sylvie the next morning at breakfast?

4. What makes the girls concerned that Sylvie might not stay?

5. What is the impression the girls have of Sylvie when they follow her into town?

6. Why do Nona and Lily make a fuss of Sylvie when she returns from her morning walk?

7. '... and we and the house were Sylvie's.' What do those final words mean?

8. What memories do the girls have of their parents, Helen and Reginald Stone?

9. What do they learn about their parents from Sylvie?

10. Using Sylvie's comments and the memories of Lucille and Ruth, write a character sketch of Helen Stone, the girls' mother.

11. Write down your own impression of Sylvie, using quotes from the text to justify your opinion of her.

Hint

How will you show which words or sentences are quotes? Look at this book for examples of quoted text.

Read and Analyse

1. There is a sense of movement and change throughout the text. For example, 'Sylvie had her coat on and appeared so very transient'. Use a dictionary to investigate words with the 'trans' prefix.

> **Example**
> *transient* – fleeting, impermanent

2. '… the wind was <u>badgering</u> the house, <u>throwing</u> frozen rain against the windows.' Find other verbs in the text which end in 'ing'. Use them in sentences of your own.

3. 'I saw the three of us posed in all the open doors of an endless train of freight cars – innumerable, rapid, identical images that produced a flickering illusion of both movement and stasis, as the pictures in a kinetoscope do.'

Write a descriptive passage which gives a sense of movement. It could be about someone hurrying to catch a train or the experience of being on a moving vehicle.

Hint
Use your word investigation.

Read, Discuss and Act

1. '… she was fastidious about washing her hands … when shy she scratched her knee.' This is the way Ruth describes some of Lucille's habits or character traits. What habits or character traits have you got?

Work in a small group to produce some imaginary characters. Who are they? Where do they live? Where do they work? What sort of habits or character traits have they got?

Now imagine that the characters are all together in a moving lift which suddenly stops. How do the characters react to this situation? Role-play their reactions and the conversations which develop. How does the scene conclude?

Warlands

by Rachel Anderson

There have been many stories which have used a wartime setting to develop a plot. How does a writer structure a story to show the effects of war on an individual? In Rachel Anderson's book *Warlands*, the story of a Vietnamese orphan, born among the bombings and terrors of war, is told by a series of bedtime stories to a little girl called Amy. The orphan was adopted by her family and Amy knows him as Uncle Ho. How Uncle Ho becomes the man she knows is explained to her through her grandmother's stories and the stories of other members of her family.

Amy

Once upon a time, not so long ago, a girl was staying with her grandmother during half-term. She was watching television. Then the news came on.

'Nearly bedtime, Amy,' called the grandmother.

'Granny, what are all those people doing?' the girl asked. On the screen she saw men and women shuffling and scrabbling to climb up onto a truck. She saw armed soldiers pushing them. She saw children crying. She saw a baby sitting by the dusty road alone, not doing anything.

'They're refugees from the war.'

'What's happening to them?'

'They're being taken to a place of safety.'

'I saw a baby. It was on its own.'

'Poor wee mite. It's probably been orphaned.'

'What's that?'

'It means when both parents are dead, so there's no one to take care of it.'

Amy thought that sounded rather exciting, to be alone in the world with nobody telling you what to do.

Her grandmother said, 'Like your Uncle Ho. He was an orphan.'

'But *he's* not a child!' said Amy indignantly. 'He's got you and Grandad.'

Although Uncle Ho was a man, he still needed quite a lot of looking after, sometimes more than Amy.

Her grandmother said, 'Yes, but Ho didn't always have us. There was a time when he had no one.'

Amy said, 'So what'll happen to that baby on the telly?'

'I expect someone will come and get him.'

'Like you got Uncle Ho?'

'Perhaps.'

The news ended. Another programme started.

'Come along now, Amy. Upstairs.'

When she was tucked up in bed, Amy remembered the war-baby on the telly and felt a very tiny bit sad for it, though not so sad that she didn't want a bedtime story. She asked her grandmother to tell her one of her special long-ago stories.

'And which ones are those?' asked her grandmother.

'Like you said you used to tell Uncle Ho when he screamed and screamed all through the night.'

'That was such a long time ago, my dear. I'm not sure I can remember them.'

'Oh, Granny. Please try.'

'Very well, dear, Which one did you want?'

'All of them. From the very beginning until you get to the end.'

'But that would take us from now till breakfast time,' said the grandmother. 'And besides, I'm not sure if there is an end yet.'

'Why isn't there?'

'Because Uncle Ho is alive and well and sitting downstairs, that's why. As you know very well.'

'All right then. Just tell me the first one. I love that one. How they found him in the gutter.' It was such a peculiar place to be found. Nobody with any sense would allow themselves to get put in a filthy gutter.

'Very well, Amy. But then you must promise, promise to go straight to sleep and no nonsense.'

''Course I will. I always do when I'm staying with you, because you're the best grandmother there ever was.' Amy sometimes told her other grandmother the same thing because she liked to keep her bread buttered on both sides.

In a Faraway Place

Once upon a time, quite a long time ago, in a beautiful faraway city where scarlet-flowering trees grew along the wide streets, and where tropical sunsets reddened the evening skies, a small child was lying in a gutter. It was late. Most people had long since hurried home and closed their shutters to be safe from raids and thieves and army patrols.

One tired policeman cycled slowly through the fruit market towards his home. He was off duty. All day he had been directing traffic and keeping an eye out for pickpockets.

As he pedalled along the boulevard beneath the flowering flame trees, he heard a frail squeaking sound. He thought it was his bike. He stopped to check the wheels. But the noise continued.

'Meeeew, meeeew.'

The policeman said to himself, 'Hmm, that's funny. It sounds a bit like a newborn kitten.'

He glanced round. He saw, lying on the ground in amongst a pile of market rubbish, a baby. It had huge brown eyes, and a mass of black hair sprouting upwards like spiky bamboo shoots.

The policeman bent down for a closer look. The baby was naked, dirty, and so thin its ribs showed under its skin like little twigs. It was a boy.

'Meeew, meeew,' the baby went, though there were no tears when it cried.

When the policeman picked it up, it wasn't heavy for it was little more than a bundle of skin and bones. He searched the nearby streets for someone to hand it back to. But there was no one.

In those days, in that faraway country, finding an abandoned child in the street was not unusual, for there was a war which had been going on for years and years, ever since the policeman had been a schoolboy. Sometimes, children's parents were killed, sometimes they went off into the forests to join the fighting, sometimes they simply ran away from their children because they had no more food and no more love to give them.

Babies were sometimes left with a scrap of paper giving their name. This one had nothing, not even a scrap of cloth for a nappy.

When the policeman found no one to pass the child on to, he heaped up some of the dry rubbish into a comfy nest and he replaced the baby on the pavement. The baby blinked its big brown eyes. It waved its thin scraggy arms and twitched its scrappy little legs.

The policeman said to himself, 'I must get home to my own little boys. My wife will start wondering where I am if I'm late. She'll be so worried. She'll think I've been stopped at a roadblock or trapped by the curfew.'

But as he pedalled away, he could hear the baby's frail mewing following him down the road.

He slowed down. He stopped.

No, no, no, he thought. I cannot leave that baby there, even if it does look as ugly as a skinned rat.

So he turned back and gathered it up out of the rubbish.

'Upon the souls of my ancestors, I do not know what I am to do with you now,' he said, holding it uncertainly. 'However, since it was your Fate that you should be left lying in the gutter, and it was my Fate that I should be the one to find you, then it is Fate that will resolve the outcome.'

And, even though the baby was dirty and damp with pee, he tucked it inside the front of his uniform jacket. 'But I really cannot take you home with me. I've five hungry children of my own.'

Because of the war, there were many shortages. There was hardly enough food for the policeman's own sons, his wife, his mother, and his mother-in-law, let alone for an extra one, however small it was.

Just then came the screaming of jets flying in low over the city. You could hear them from a long way off.

EEEEEEeeeeeeeeeeeee.

They were going to bomb the villages hidden in the deep green forests beyond the city. When they hit a target, there was another sound, bom bom bom, and the ground shook.

Some people said you grew used to it. But the policeman didn't think that the sound of people and homes being smashed was something you ever got used to.

He ran with the baby to one of the round concrete drains that were used as shelters. Sometimes bombs fell short of their targets and hit the city instead. He crouched in the drain until the raid was over and it was safe to hurry home. But the policeman couldn't go to his home yet. He still had the mewing infant tucked in the front of his jacket.

He walked slowly through the deserted market place, pushing his bike with one hand, supporting the baby with the other, wishing he could get rid of it to someone else. But these days everybody had troubles enough of their own.

He came to a broken-down building. It had a roughly painted sign propped on the tin roof which said *Hoi Duc Anh*. Although he went past here nearly every day, he'd never before given it a second thought. *Hoi Duc Anh* meant *The Association for the Protection of Infants*. It was a place where children who had got no one to look after them could stay.

Why, of course! thought the policeman. It is Fate that I have come this way.

The orphanage had once been used as a school. A grumpy-looking old woman was about to secure the main gate for the night with a padlock and chain.

'Yes?' she said sharply. 'What is it?'

The policeman took the dirty child from his jacket and held it out for her. 'I found this,' he said. 'Near the fruit market. Just beyond the fish market.'

'Name?'

The policeman shrugged. 'I have no idea.'

'Then you should have looked for its parents.'

'I did. There was no one.'

'Well, you people can't expect to hand in every abondoned baby you find, just like that. We've got more than enough as it is. Can't you hear them?'

Indeed the policeman could. The distant wailing and grizzling and greeting and crying of a hundred or more sad babies' voices was almost worse than the screaming of an air-raid.

He said, 'I really must be on my way. My wife will be worried.'

'I'm not interested in all that,' said the woman. 'I've got more than enough worries here. If citizens bring in lost babies, I have to follow the proper procedure. Your name, and your address, if you please. I'll fetch the book.' She unlocked the gate and beckoned him into the compound.

'*My* name? Why mine?'

'We have to make sure he's really a stray, and not one of your own that you can't be bothered with. People do that. Then, as soon as we've fattened them up, they reclaim them.'

She left the policeman standing on the verandah of the orphanage while she went off to find her registration book. He waited. And waited.

What am I to do now? the policeman wondered. I really can't stay here all night, and then wait some more while she asks me questions about my name and address. And if I do give her my address, she may hold me responsible for this orphan boy's future welfare. All I need is to be sure that he has a safe place to sleep tonight. I won't wait around another moment for that woman.

So he laid the baby in a big broken wicker chair in the corner by the door where the woman could not fail to notice him when she returned.

'I have done the best that I can,' said the policeman to himself as he climbed onto his bike and pedalled away. 'At least the boy will now sleep with a roof over his head.'

In fact, the rusty tin roof of the orphanage had holes in it that let in the rain. And there were many fat happy rats that lived in the rafters. But the policeman was not to know that.

The baby lying in the wicker chair put his fist into his mouth and began to gnaw and mew at the same time.

When the woman came back with her big book, she was irritated to find the man had gone.

'Oh my, what a to-do. Where's the fellow that brought you in? This is absurd, just dumping you here. It really won't do. But that's what they all do these days. No civic responsibility.'

The baby stared without seeing. He was now so tired and so hungry that he couldn't even be bothered to make the squeaky mewing noise.

'Oh, all right then, you,' the woman grumbled, and she picked him up, not very gently. 'You can stay. But just look at the sight of you, no clothes, covered in scabs, scraggy as a wet dog. *And* you've piddled all over the chair!'

She carried him to a bleak room more like a shed, where there were a hundred and more children and babies. Fifty smaller ones lay down one side of the room on newspaper and blankets. Fifty-three older ones were contained in wire cots down the other side.

What a din and what a smell there was in that place. But at least there was a roof over everybody's heads and a chance of being fed. The orphanage had cartons of powdered milk and feeding bottles, though not enough of either to go round one hundred and three people. Each child had its brief turn. When their time was up, the dribbling teat was pulled from their lips and thrust into the next mouth in the line.

The grumpy woman wrapped a piece of torn cotton cloth round the latest arrival and laid him on the newspaper with the others to wait for his turn.

The next morning, in the office of the orphanage, the woman opened up the big book to fill in the details.

'We got a new boy handed in last evening,' she told one of the younger women who came to help at the *Hoi Duc Anh*. 'Picked up by a traffic policeman. The child looked near death last night. Didn't think he'd be alive by morning. But he's hanging on. If he lives, he'll have to have a name.'

Read, Think and Write

1. How does Amy first become aware of the effects of war?

2. What does Amy think about the idea of being an orphan?

3. Where was Uncle Ho found and who found him?

4. Give three reasons why children were often abandoned.

5. Why does the policeman not take the baby home with him?

6. 'Just then came the screaming of jets flying in low over the city.' What does the policeman feel about the air raid?

7. Where does the policeman leave the baby?

8. 'A grumpy-looking old woman was about to secure the main gate for the night …' Find examples from the text to show the way the woman feels about the arrival of the baby.

> **Example**
> 'Yes?' she said <u>sharply</u>.

9. Compare the way the author describes the baby when the policeman first finds it with the impression that the woman at the orphanage has of it.

10. Describe the conditions in the orphanage.

11. Using the style of a report by a war correspondent for a newspaper, rewrite the events narrated in the grandmother's story, 'In a Faraway Place'.

Read and Analyse

1. At the beginning of the extract, Amy and her grandmother are having a conversation in front of the television. Find the section where the writer does not use verbs of speech or names to indicate who is speaking. Write out this section, adding the name of the speaker and a suitable verb and adverb.

> **Example**
> 'They're refugees from the war,' explained the grandmother patiently.

2. Find synonyms for the noun 'peace' and the adjective 'peaceful'. Find synonyms for the noun 'war'.

3. Look at the first paragraph of grandmother's bedtime story – 'In a Faraway Place'. How many sentences are there? Which words in the first sentence make the setting sound peaceful? Which words in the third sentence make the setting threatening and unwelcome? Notice how the short sentence in between helps change the tone. Use the paragraph as a model to write two complex sentences that show the contrast between the peacefulness before an air raid and the chaos during the raid. Change the tone by using a short sentence.

Hint
Go back and look at your synonym investigation.

Read, Discuss and Act

1. Do you think news programmes which show real people trying to cope in war-torn countries help us to understand how they feel? Do we need fictional war stories when we can see the facts?

2. Role-play a scene showing the policeman and the woman who runs the orphanage being interviewed by a reporter for a television news programme.

Moby Dick

by Herman Melville, retold by Geraldine McCaughrean

Herman Melville's novel was first published under the title 'The Whale' in 1851. The following extract is taken from a retelling of the story by Geraldine McCaughrean. A retelling may involve adjustments to detail because of the style of language used, but the conflicts and resolutions of the plot should remain the same.

2
The Gold Dubloon

Ships like the *Pequod* are not owned by one fat tycoon rubbing his soft hands in some New York counting house. Nor are they owned by their captains. Whole towns own them – a plank here, a nail there. Widows and retired sailors, clergymen and chandlers, thrifty shopkeepers and destitute orphanages may all own tiny shares in a single Nantucket whaler. So when it puts out to sea, a whole community of souls watches it go. They watch their investment sail over the horizon, and watch from the hilltops to see it sail home again: their means of survival. A lot was resting on the success of our voyage.

We sailed on Christmas morning, the sun still resting on the morning clouds like Jesus on his manger of straw. And still I had not set eyes on the mysterious Captain Ahab. He kept belowdecks, and the longer he remained invisible, the greater our awe of him grew. His cabin was like some holy shrine where no man entered – nor would have dared to enter, for fear of meeting God.

We heard him, though. At night, swinging in our hammocks, we could head Ahab walking the deck overhead, up and down, up and down. A soft thud was followed by a sharp crack: a man's foot and then the sharp tap of a peg. For Captain Ahab had only one leg.

I heard Starbuck say to him once, 'Wilt thou not rest, captain? Thou wakest the men from sleep with the clatter of thy leg.'

The answer came back no louder than the growl of a sleeping bear: 'Why should they sleep? Do I sleep? Besides … the sound of my whalebone leg will trample dreams of whales into their sleeping brains, and what business have they to sleep unless it's to dream of whales?'

I looked around me, in the creaking tarry dark. The words of the madman, Elijah, kept coming back to me. Who were the 'demons' Elijah had said were Ahab's travelling companions? These men snoring in their hammocks? Surely not. Exotic, yes, but demons? The meanest of the lot was the God-fearing Bildad, who knew every verse of the Bible, which gave him the excuse to be a skinflint. He gripped his moneybags tight to his chest and never spent a red cent if he could help it. Even now his head was resting on a pillow full of pennies. He deserved a stiff neck, but not to be called a demon.

Then there was Tashtego, whose glossy, purple-black hair was as long as a woman's: a pure-breed American Indian whose forefathers had hunted moose with bow-and-arrow.

Daggoo was a coal-black African, whose only wealth was the gold in his two huge ear-rings. Nobody in their right mind would have tried to steal them: Daggoo was as big as a bull and tall as a giraffe. But he was no demon.

There were men from the Azores, from Greenland, Shetland, and Wales, but though they were colourful barbarians, no one with an ounce of charity could have called them demons. I concluded that Mister Elijah was a half-wit and his talk of demons nothing but gibberish.

For three weeks, Ahab kept to his cabin. Then suddenly one day we look up and he was there – above us on the quarterdeck – a long, lean man all in black but for the white of his whalebone peg-leg. His eyes barely showed, for the sockets had faced for so many years into sun and wind that they were screwed into a tangle of creases. The face was long and expressionless, like those monumental faces carved into the hillsides of Easter Island. Weathered into premature old age, Ahab's face was marred, too, by a scar which ran from the hairline down one cheek and in at the collar, as if it

might run down as far as his feet. It looked as if our captain had been split in two and sewn carefully back together with needle and thread; or made, perhaps, from the halves of two different men. Inserting the tip of his whalebone leg into a hole in the deck, he perfected his balance, then leaned towards us over the quarterdeck rail and bellowed, 'Tell me, men! What d'you do if you see a whale?'

'*Shout out, sir!*' we bellowed back at him.

'Then what?'

'*We lower the boats and go after him, sir!*'

Ahab looked ferociously gratified. He reached upwards, as if to snatch the trailing edge of a sail, but he had something in his hand. 'Here's an ounce of Spanish gold!' he declared. 'A sixteen-dollar piece! D'you see it? Mister Starbuck, pass me that mallet!' He placed the huge glittering coin against the main mast, as high as he could reach, and drove a nail through its soft, pure gold circle. 'This is for the man who wins me a certain white whale. You'll know it when you see it. It has a wrinkled forehead and a crooked jaw. There are three holes in its starboard fluke, and a twisted harpoon in its hump. That's mine, that harpoon.'

'I have seen this white whale,' murmured Queequeg from close behind me. 'Last voyage. I put harpoon in, but he pulled loose.'

'I must have that whale, men! I will have him!'

'You mean Moby Dick, don't you, captain?' shouted Tashtego.

'Moby Dick, yes!'

'Wasn't it he that took thy leg, captain?' said Starbuck quietly from close by Ahab's shoulder, but Ahab answered as if we had all taunted him with the loss, and glared.

'Who told you that? Yes! He's the beast that took off my leg, and turned me into this stumbling cripple of a half-man … But now I'm part-whale, aren't I? Like him. Next time I'll make him pay. I'll chase him round the Cape of Good Hope and round Cape Horn, if I have to! We'll chase him from Norway to the Equator, and over all the sides of the Earth, till he spouts black blood. What d'you say, shipmates?'

It was thrilling talk. We were all on tiptoe, already looking out to sea, swearing death to the white whale as if it had eaten our own mothers. Sixteen dollars is a year's wage to most men, and each of us was inwardly spending that gold dubloon, cent by quarter. I know I was.

Only Starbuck, the first mate, had a look on his face like Low Sunday. Ahab saw it. 'What's your trouble, Quaker?' he growled, teetering slightly off balance. 'Too risky an enterprise for you?'

'Oh, I'll risk anything for enterprise,' said Starbuck. 'I'll follow the harpoon into the whale's mouth to be sure of getting its oil. That's my business. Oil. That's what we're here for. To turn a profit, taking oil. But revenge? Where's the profit in that? How many barrels of oil wilt revenge stow in the hold?'

Ahab rocked his big head from side to side and bared his teeth in a humourless grin. 'Oh, *money*! Is that what's worrying you, Mister Starbuck? Well, if money's the be-all and end-all, this planet of ours belongs to the book-keepers, and the stars are only hung up there to be counted and banked! But if it's any business of yours, Quaker, my revenge will make me richer *here*.' And he banged his chest.

Starbuck seemed more horrified than ever. 'Chase a dumb beast, to punish it for a crime it committed out of blind instinct? That's nigh blasphemous. It's mad, if thou ask me.'

Ahab swivelled round on his whalebone pivot, swelling with rage like a black sail full of wind. He jabbed at Starbuck with the fingers of both hands, his spittle flying in the man's face, his voice so loud that the mate winced and flinched away from it.

'Blasphemous? I'd pull the sun down out of the sky, if it insulted me!' roared Ahab. 'And that hulking fish insults me. Its very *existence* insults me. It's white, isn't it? Everything man fears is the colour of that whale. Ghosts, shrouds, masks; things invisible; blind things under the earth. White's a zero. It's someone who ought to be there and isn't; a blind man's eye without a pupil in it; icebergs reaching under the water to claw the hull out of my ship. What is it out there, that lump of mystery? Do you know? Can you tell me? It's the *mystery* of him that screws me in knots. It torments me. He provokes me. I'm like a man in prison and he's the wall – the wall I have to smash down to get free! He's a white mask, and I don't know whose face is on the other side, laughing at me. Whose is it? Can you tell me? Don't you understand anything? We have to smash away the mask. We have to *know*, d'you see? *All the answers.*'

The two men stood frozen, their faces so close they must have been breathing each other's breaths. Starbuck was pale – whale white with shock, bludgeoned half unconscious with words, like a man set upon by thugs. A wicked glint in Ahab's eye said that he knew he had Starbuck in his power, that they had locked horns and Starbuck had lost the trial of strength. The mate seemed to shrink, as if Ahab had shaken the very guts out of him.

Calling for grog, Captain Ahab summoned together the harpooners and filled the hollow shaft of each man's harpoon with neat liquor. He had them raise their harpoons full of rum, in a toast. He had them raise the spears into a metal spire, with his own fist at the summit, joining them. His single, burning ambition conducted itself like lightning through those joined harpoons: '*Death to Moby Dick!*'

'Death to Moby Dick!' the harpooners chorused, round-eyed, like children dared into doing something huge and dangerous. 'And may God hunt us all to our deaths, if we don't hunt Moby Dick to his!'

I nearly shouted it myself, but the look on Starbuck's face made me think twice. Then someone thrust the grog bottle into my hand, and I drank off a swig. It hit my stomach like fire. It hit my brain like a fist. '*Death to Moby Dick!*' I crowed, the little cook-boy Pip shook his tambourine in my ear and jangled away all my doubts. Here was a thing worth doing – to hunt a monster round the planet and rid the sea of it, like Theseus killing the Minotaur, like Perseus killing the Gorgon, like George killing the dragon. '*Death to Moby Dick!*'

The sun shone on the gold dubloon so brightly that I could hardly bear to look at it. Death to Moby Dick and sixteen dollars to me. No doubt about it.

Then someone started to dance, and soon we were all dancing, while Ahab, up on his quarterdeck, stretched out hands over us in a blessing. Or like the puppeteer pulling our strings.

Read, Think and Write

1. How is the ship *Pequod* described in the first paragraph to show the different concerns for a successful voyage?

2. How long is it before the crew see Captain Ahab?

3. What were the names of six of the narrator's travelling companions?

4. What reward does Ahab offer his crew for winning him a 'certain white whale' and where does he place the reward?

5. Why is it so important to Ahab to hunt for Moby Dick?

6. What is important to Starbuck?

7. How does Ahab make Moby Dick sound like a monster that should be feared?

8. What other monsters are mentioned in the extract?

9. At first, the narrator does not join in with the shout 'Death to Moby Dick'. Why is he unsure? What makes him change his mind?

10. Write down examples of how the writer describes Captain Ahab's appearance.

11. The main conflict to be resolved in the plot is Ahab's revenge on Moby Dick. There is also a conflict between Starbuck and Ahab. How does the writer show this in the extract?

12. Retell this extract in your own words, making sure the main elements of the plot are clear.

Hint
Make a list of the main points in the extract and put them in order as a frame for your retelling.

Read and Analyse

1. Find examples in the text of the use of colons. Which of the following purposes are they used for?
   (a) To introduce lists.
   (b) To introduce speech and quotations.
   (c) To explain, expand or summarise.
   Write sentences of your own showing the different uses of the colon.

2. Fear, mask, claw, colour
   Write sentences for these words from the text, using each word both as a noun and as a verb.

   > **Example**
   > They were trembling with fear.
   > 'I fear Moby Dick,' he said.

3. Using the extract to help you, write a conversation between Starbuck and Ahab in playscript form.

Hint
Remember the different uses of colons.

Read, Discuss and Act

1. 'Oh, *money!* Is that what's worrying you, Mister Starbuck? Well, if money's the be-all and end-all, this planet of ours belongs to the book-keepers, and the stars are only hung up there to be counted and banked!'

   What does Ahab mean by this? Do you agree?

2. 'It was thrilling talk. We were all on tiptoe, already looking out to sea, swearing death to the white whale as if it had eaten our own mothers.'

   Ahab is very persuasive. With a partner or in a small group, act out a scene where you are trying to persuade someone to see your point of view. You might be trying to convince someone of a personal belief, such as Ahab's desire for revenge. Or you might be engaged in an enterprise for profit, such as a salesperson demonstrating a vacuum cleaner or a market trader selling an assortment of goods from their stall. Make your character either obsessive and fanatical or grimly determined.

75

The Amber Spyglass

by Philip Pullman

Philip Pullman has developed a plot to span all three books in the trilogy *His Dark Materials*. The first two books are entitled *Northern Lights* and *The Subtle Knife*. This extract is taken from the final book of the trilogy, *The Amber Spyglass*. The narrative has been woven into many conflicts and resolutions, unlike a short story which may have just one conflict to be resolved. The main character, who moves through the plot of all three books, is a young girl called Lyra. She has the rare skill of being able to read an alethiometer, a symbol machine which can help give insight into future events. The characters are able to move from one world to another through 'windows' which can be cut by 'a subtle knife'.

Dr Mary Malone, a scientist and a friend of Lyra, is trying to help the mulefa, who are threatened with extinction. Father Gomez is tracking Dr Malone as part of a campaign to murder Lyra.

27
The Platform

My soul into the boughs does glide:
There like a bird it sits, and sings,
Then whets, and combs its silver wings …
Andrew Marvell

Once the mulefa began to build the platform for Mary, they worked quickly and well. She enjoyed watching them, because they could discuss without quarrelling and co-operate without getting in each other's way, and because their techniques of splitting and cutting and joining wood were so elegant and effective.

Within two days, the observation platform was designed and built and lifted into place. It was firm and spacious and comfortable, and when she had climbed up to it she was as happy, in one way, as she had ever been. That one way was physically. In the dense green of the canopy, with the rich blue of the sky between the leaves; with a breeze keeping her skin cool, and the faint scent of the flowers delighting her whenever she sensed it; with the rustle of the leaves, the song of the hundreds of birds, and the distant murmur of the waves on the seashore, all her senses were lulled and nurtured, and if she could have stopped thinking, she would have been entirely lapped in bliss.

But of course thinking was what she was there for.

And when she looked through her spyglass and saw the relentless outward drift of the sraf, the Shadow-particles, it seemed to her as if happiness and life and hope were drifting away with them. She could find no explanation at all.

Three hundred years, the mulefa had said: that was how long the trees had been failing. Given that the Shadow-particles passed through all the worlds alike, presumably the same thing was happening in her universe too, and in every other one. Three hundred years ago, the Royal Society was set up: the first true scientific society in her world. Newton was making his discoveries about optics and gravitation.

Three hundred years ago in Lyra's world, someone invented the alethiometer.

At the same time in that strange world through which she'd come to get here, the subtle knife was invented.

She lay back on the planks, feeling the platform move in a very slight, very slow rhythm as the great tree swayed in the sea-breeze. Holding the spyglass to her eye, she watched the myriad tiny sparkles drift through the leaves, past the open mouths of the blossoms, through the massive boughs, moving against the wind, in a slow deliberate current that looked all but conscious.

What had happened three hundred years ago? Was it the cause of the Dust-current, or was it the other way round? Or were they both the results of a different cause altogether? Or were they simply not connected at all?

The drift was mesmerizing. How easy it would be to fall into a trance, and let her mind drift away with the floating particles …

Before she knew what she was doing, and because her body was lulled, that was exactly what happened. She suddenly snapped awake to find herself outside her body, and she panicked.

She was a little way above the platform, and a few feet off among the branches. And something had happened to the Dust-wind: instead of that slow drift, it was racing like a river in flood. Had it speeded up, or was time moving differently for her, now she was outside her body? Either way, she was conscious of the most horrible danger, because the flood was threatening to sweep her loose completely, and it was immense. She flung out her arms to seize hold of anything solid – but she had no arms. Nothing connected. Now she was almost over that abominable drop, and her body was further and further from reach, sleeping so hoggishly below her. She tried to shout and wake herself up: not a sound. The body slumbered on, and the self that observed was being borne away out of the canopy of leaves altogether and into the open sky.

And no matter how she struggled she could make no headway. The force that carried her out was as smooth and powerful as water pouring over a weir: the particles of Dust were streaming along as if they too were pouring over some invisible edge.

And carrying her away from her body.

She flung a mental lifeline to that physical self, and tried to recall the feeling of being in it: all the sensations that made up being alive. The exact touch of her friend Atal's soft-tipped trunk caressing her neck. The taste of bacon and eggs. The triumphant strain in her muscles as she pulled herself up a rockface. The delicate dancing of her fingers on a computer keyboard. The smell of roasting coffee. The warmth of her bed on a winter night.

And gradually she stopped moving; the lifeline held fast, and she felt the weight and strength of the current pushing against her as she hung there in the sky.

And then a strange thing happened. Little by little (as she reinforced those sense-memories, adding others: tasting an iced Margarita in California, sitting under the lemon trees outside a restaurant in Lisbon, scraping the frost off the windscreen of her car) she felt the Dust-wind easing. The pressure was lessening.

But only on *her*: all around, above and below, the great flood was streaming as fast as ever. Somehow there was a little patch of stillness around her, where the particles were resisting the flow.

They *were* conscious! They felt her anxiety, and responded to it. And they began to carry her back to her deserted body, and when she was close enough to see it once more, so heavy, so warm, so safe, a silent sob convulsed her heart.

And then she sank back into her body, and awoke.

She took in a deep shuddering breath. She pressed her hands and her legs against the rough planks of the platform, and having a minute ago nearly gone mad with fear, she was now suffused with a deep slow ecstasy at being one with her body and the earth and everything that was matter.

Finally she sat up and tried to take stock. Her fingers found the spyglass, and she held it to her eye, supporting one trembling hand with the other. There was no doubt about it: that slow sky-wide drift had become a flood. There was nothing to hear and nothing to feel, and without the spyglass, nothing to see, but even when she took the glass from her eye, the sense of that swift silent inundation remained vividly, together with something she hadn't noticed in the terror of being outside her body: the profound, helpless regret that was abroad in the air.

The Shadow-particles knew what was happening, and were sorrowful.

And she herself was partly Shadow-matter. Part of her was subject to this tide that was moving through the cosmos. And so were the mulefa, and so were human beings in every world, and every kind of conscious creature, wherever they were.

And unless she found out what was happening, they might all find themselves drifting away to oblivion, every one.

Suddenly she longed for the earth again. She put the spyglass in her pocket and began the long climb down to the ground.

Father Gomez stepped through the window as the evening light lengthened and mellowed, He saw the great stands of wheel-trees and the roads lacing through the prairie, just as Mary had done from the same spot some time before. But the air was free of haze, for it had rained a little earlier, and he could see further than she had; in particular, he could see the glimmer of a distant sea, and some flickering white shapes that might be sails.

He lifted the rucksack higher on his shoulders, and turned towards them, to see what he could find. In the calm of the long evening it was pleasant to walk on this smooth road, with the sound of some cicada-like creatures in the long grass and the setting sun warm in his face. The air was fresh, too, clear and sweet and entirely free of the taint of naphtha-fumes, kerosene-fumes, whatever they were, which had lain so heavily on the air in one of the worlds he'd passed through: the world his target, the tempter herself, belonged to.

He came out at sunset on a little headland beside a shallow bay. If they had tides in this sea, the tide was high, because there was only a narrow fringe of soft white sand above the water.

And floating in the calm bay were a dozen or more … Father Gomez had to stop and think carefully. A dozen or more enormous snow-white birds, each the size of a rowing-boat, with long straight wings which trailed on the water behind them: very long wings, six feet or more in length. *Were* they birds? They had feathers, and heads and beaks not unlike swans', but those wings were situated one in front of the other, surely …

Suddenly they saw him. Heads turned with a snap, and at once all those wings were raised high, exactly like the sails of a yacht, and they all leaned in with the breeze, making for the shore.

Father Gomez was impressed by the beauty of those wing-sails, by how they were flexed and trimmed so perfectly, and by the speed of the birds. Then he saw that they were paddling, too: they had legs under the water, placed not fore-and-aft like the wings but side by side, and with the wings and the legs together, they had an extraordinary speed and grace in the water.

As the first one reached the shore it lumbered up through the dry sand, making directly for the priest. It was hissing with malice, stabbing its head forward as it waddled heavily up the shore, and the beak snapped and clacked. There were teeth in the beak, too, like a series of sharp incurved hooks.

Father Gomez was about a hundred yards from the edge of the water, on a low grassy promontory, and he had plenty of time to put down his rucksack, take out the rifle, load and aim and fire.

The bird's head exploded in a mist of red and white, and the dead creature blundered on clumsily for several steps before sinking on to its breast. It didn't die for a minute or more; the legs kicked, the wings rose and fell, and the great bird beat itself round and round in a bloody circle, kicking up the rough grass, until a long bubbling expiration from its lungs ended with a coughing spray of red, and it fell still.

The other birds had stopped as soon as the first one fell, and stood watching it, and watching the man, too. There was a quick ferocious intelligence in their eyes. They looked from him to the dead bird, from that to the rifle, from the rifle to his face.

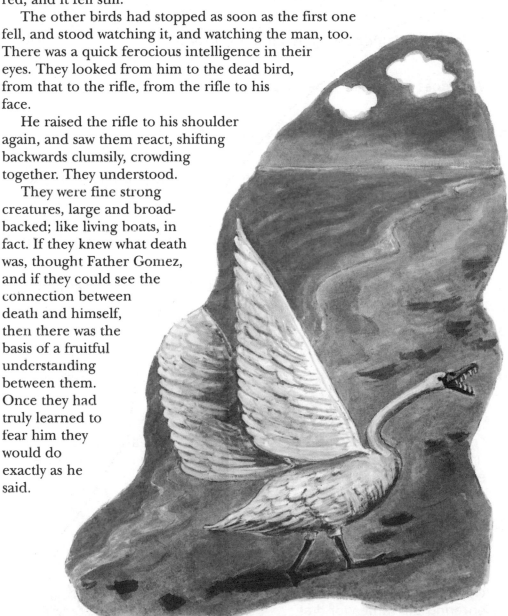

He raised the rifle to his shoulder again, and saw them react, shifting backwards clumsily, crowding together. They understood.

They were fine strong creatures, large and broad-backed; like living boats, in fact. If they knew what death was, thought Father Gomez, and if they could see the connection between death and himself, then there was the basis of a fruitful understanding between them. Once they had truly learned to fear him they would do exactly as he said.

Read, Think and Write

1. What are the mulefa doing at the beginning of the extract and how do their actions show what sort of creatures they are?

2. What are the discoveries that happened three hundred years ago which have been important to the plot of the story?

3. What is Dr Malone doing up on the platform?

4. Why does she panic? What happens to her?

5. What does she do in order to save herself?

6. Why is it important that Dr Malone finds out what is happening to the Shadow-particles?

7. What impression does Father Gomez have of the world he steps into?

8. What action does he take when one of the birds approaches him?

9. How do the other birds react to his action?

10. What was the basis of 'a fruitful understanding' between Father Gomez and the birds?

11. Following a sequence of events is important in creating and understanding the plot of a story. Write down the main sequence of events in this extract.

12. Some events do not have an immediate resolution but are resolved later in the plot. What do you think the effect will be of Father Gomez entering the same world as Dr Malone?

Hint
Design a suitable writing frame or a format to display the plot sequence, using headings, arrows, bullet points, etc.

1. Find examples in the text of the use of semi-colons. Which of the following purposes are they used for?
   (a) To separate closely related statements.
   (b) To separate contrasting statements.
   (c) To introduce long or complicated lists.
   Write five sentences of your own using semicolons.

2. Find examples from the text to show how the author has described sensations of sound, smell, sight and touch.

   > **Example**
   > 'The delicate dancing of her fingers on a computer keyboard.'

3. Imagine you have just walked through a window into another world. Write a descriptive passage giving impressions of the sensations of sound, smell, sight and touch.

1. Dr Malone is a scientist and is trying to understand the dust current she is observing. Scientists like Stephen Hawking are studying the forces and particles of matter in this universe. Do you think there might be other worlds? What might be the effects on our world if there were? Share and discuss your impressions of possible other worlds.

2. What scientific discoveries do you think have been important? Have there been discoveries that might create problems? On your own or with a partner, prepare and give a short talk on a discovery that you think is important. Explain what you think the effects of this discovery have been and how it might perhaps be developed in the future.

3. Scientists are often stereotyped as rather eccentric characters ('the mad scientist'). In a small group, develop a scene where an eccentric scientist and his/her incompetent assistant are trying to explain and demonstrate what they feel is an important discovery.

Crossing Over

by Catherine Storr

The Kitchen

by David Almond

A fascination with the paranormal has made the ghost story a continually popular genre. It is a genre that has attracted a wide variety of writers over time. Some writers have chosen to use the form to amuse, others have used it to frighten or to leave the reader wondering.

Catherine Storr has developed the plot of this story using a very ordinary situation and setting. She does not give the girl in the story a name but it is through what the girl thinks and feels that she tells the story.

'The Kitchen' is from a collection of stories which David Almond wrote about his childhood. As he says in his introduction, 'like all stories they merge memory and dream, the real and the imagined, truth and lies.'

Crossing Over

If she hadn't been fond of dogs, she would never have volunteered for this particular job. When her class at school were asked if they would give up some of their spare time towards helping old people, most of the tasks on offer had sounded dreary. Visiting housebound old men and women, making them cups of tea and talking to them; she hadn't fancied that, and she wasn't any good at making conversation, let alone being able to shout loud enough for a deaf person to hear. Her voice was naturally quiet. She didn't like the idea of doing anyone else's shopping, she wasn't good enough at checking that she'd got the right change. The check-out girls in the supermarket were too quick, ringing up the different items on the cash register. Nor did she want to push a wheelchair to the park. But walking old Mrs Matthews' dog, that had seemed like something she might even enjoy. She couldn't go every evening, but she would take him for a good long run on the Common on Saturdays, and on fine evenings, when the days were longer, she'd try to call for him after school some weekdays. She had started out full of enthusiasm.

What she hadn't reckoned with was the dog himself. Togo was huge, half Alsatian, half something else which had given him long woolly hair, permanently matted and dirty. Once, right at the beginning, she had offered to bathe and groom him, but Mrs Matthews had been outraged by the suggestion, was sure the poor creature would catch cold, and at the sight of the comb Togo backed and growled and showed his teeth. It was as much as she could do to fasten and unfasten his leash, and he did not make that easy. The early evening walks weren't quite so bad, because there wasn't time to take him to the Common, so he stayed on the leash all the time. Even then he was difficult to manage. He seemed to have had no training and he certainly had no manners. He never stopped when she told him to, never came when she called him, so that every Saturday, when she dutifully let him run free among the gorse bushes and little trees on the Common, she was afraid she might have to return to Mrs Matthews without the dog, confessing that he had run away. Mrs Matthews did not admit that Togo was unruly and difficult to manage, any more than she would admit that he smelled. It was only a feeling that she shouldn't go back on her promise to perform this small service to the community that kept the girl still at the disagreeable task.

This particular evening was horrible. She'd been kept later at school than usual, and although it was already March, the sky was overcast, it was beginning to get dark, and a fine drizzling rain made the pavements slippery. Togo was in a worse mood than usual. He had slouched along, stopping for whole minutes at lampposts and dustbins and misbehaving extravagantly in the most inconvenient places, in spite of her frantic tugs at the leash to try to get him off the pavement. He was too strong for her to control, and he knew it. She almost believed that he had a spite against her, and enjoyed showing that he didn't have to do anything she wanted, as if it wasn't bad enough having to go out in public with an animal so unkempt and anti-social.

They reached the zebra crossing on the hill. The traffic was moving fast, as it always did during the evening rush-hour. She would have to wait for a break before she could step off the pavement, especially as, in the half dark, she knew from her Dad's comments when he was driving, pedestrians on the road were not easy to see. She stood still and dragged at Togo's lead. But Togo did not mean to be dictated to by a little schoolgirl, and after a moment's hesitation, he pulled too. He was off, into the middle of the oncoming traffic, wrenching at the leash, which she had twisted round her hand in order to get a better grip. She threw all her weight against his, but she was no match for him. She thought she felt the worn leather snap, she heard the sound of screaming brakes and someone shouted. She had time to think, 'What am I going to say to Mrs Matthews?', before her head swam and she thought she was going to faint.

She found herself standing on the further side of the road. She saw a huddle of people, surrounding stationary cars. Two drivers had left their vehicles and were abusing each other. As the crowd swayed, she saw the bonnet of a red car crumpled by its contact with the back of a large yellow van. She saw, too, a dark stain on the road surface. Blood. Blood made her feel sick and her head swam again. She hesitated, knowing that she ought to go among the watching people to make herself look, perhaps to try to explain how Togo had pulled, how she hadn't been strong enough to hold him back. Someone should be told whose dog he was. Someone would have to go and break the terrible news to Mrs Matthews.

As she was considering this, she heard the siren of a police car and the two-note call of an ambulance. She thought, 'Perhaps someone got badly hurt in one of the cars, and it's all my fault.' Her courage evaporated, and she turned away from the accident and began to walk, on legs that trembled, up the hill towards her own home. She thought, 'I'll go and tell Mum.' But then she remembered how much Mrs Matthews loved horrible Togo, how she talked about him as her only friend, and how dreadful it was going to be for her to open her front door to find a policeman telling her that her dog was dead. Besides, the policeman might say that it was her, the girl's, fault. She had to go first to Mrs Matthew's house, to break the news gently, and also to explain that she had tried her best to prevent the accident.

She found that she must have been walking really fast, which was surprising, considering how much she was dreading the ordeal in front of her. She had reached the grocer's and the newspaper shop at the top of the High Street almost before she'd realized. She saw Sybil Grainger coming out of the newspaper shop, and she was ready to say, 'Hi!' and to pretend that there was nothing wrong, but luckily Sybil seemed not to have seen her. She turned the corner into Grange Road, relieved that she hadn't had to carry on a conversation. Grange Road also seemed shorter than usual; now she had to go along Fenton Crescent till she reached the small side street where Mrs Matthews lived, in one of the row of little old cottages known as Paradise Row.

Her heart beat furiously as she unlatched the small wooden gate and walked the short distance up to the front door, rehearsing exactly how to say what she had to. She lifted the knocker. As it came down on the wood, it made a hollow, echoing sound.

Extraordinary. From the other side of the door, she heard something very much like Togo's menacing growl. She must be in such a state of nerves that she was imagining impossible things. Or perhaps when she felt faint out there in the road, she had fallen and hit her head and been concussed. She felt her scalp, under the straight, silky hair, but she couldn't find any tender spots. She waited. Mrs Matthews was arthritic and always took a long time to answer the door and there was no hurry for the message she was going to receive.

Steps came slowly, dragging a little, along the passage. The door opened, and she braced herself for the shock she was about to administer and the scolding she was certainly going to receive.

But when Mrs Matthews looked out, she behaved in a very peculiar way. Instead of saying immediately, 'Where's Togo?' she asked nothing of her visitor, but bent forward and peered out, looking up and down the short row of cottages, as if she were searching for something or someone who might be coming or going in the street. Her head with its thinning grey hair was so close that the girl stepped back, opening her mouth to begin her explanation. But what she saw in the passage behind the old woman stopped her from uttering a sound.

At the further end of the passage was a dog. Togo. Togo, whole, apparently unharmed, his collar round his neck, and the end of the broken leash still attached, dragging behind him.

For a moment she thought he was going to spring forward and attack her. Then she saw that, instead, he was backing, shrinking as far away as he could get. He was making a curious noise, not a howl, nor a growl, but a sort of whine. She noticed that he was trembling. She had never seen Togo tremble before. He was showing whites round his yellow eyes and the short hair round his muzzle was bristling.

She started to speak. But Mrs Matthews appeared not to have heard her. She was turning to calm the terrified dog. She was saying, 'Whatever's the matter with you, Togo? Think you're seeing a ghost?'

The Kitchen

The drone of the distant city, the clatter and hum of Felling nearby. In another garden, children sing a skipping song: *January, February, March, April, May …* An invisible lark high above. A blackbird calling from the apple tree. The scent of roses and warm grass. The sun burns at the centre of the sky. Light pours down into the garden, through the window, through the gap of the half-open door, through dust that seethes, dances, glitters …

And Mam smiles.

'Hm. Just look at us. Right out of space again.'

Here she is on the old white chair with a hundred holes like stars. And Dad on the low stool at her side.

'We'd have moved on to a bigger place,' he says.

'I know,' she answers. 'Yes. I know.'

And here we are, leaning against the worktops, the fridge, the sink, the little table. We drink tea and eat toast. We allow the toast to cool for a moment, so that the butter we spread melts only at its edges, so that much of it remains, bright yellow, half-solid on the crisp surface. There is cheese, lemon curd, Golden Shred. So simple, so sweet, enough for all of us.

We breathe so gently, so carefully. We don't stare. The light pours in.

Barbara wears cream trousers, a white blouse, white shoes. Her hair is cut short but it curls around her ears, it curls on her brow. Little silver earrings like teardrops. A narrow silver necklace. She stands with her left hand resting on the bench and her head tilted languidly to one side. She is so shy here, with us all around her. She keeps lowering her eyes, and her face colours gently as she smiles.

I look at Mam and she shakes her head and bites her lip: just give her time. We don't stare. The light doesn't change, the singing goes on. Catherine catches my eye.

'Nothing must happen,' she says. 'Nothing.'

Dad touches Margaret's hand.

'I was thinking,' he says. 'Do you remember? One day you said to me, Where's the smallest place in the world?'

She shakes her head.

'I don't remember,' she whispers.

'You were young.'

He smiles at Margaret and at the memory of Margaret and for a moment we all see her as she was, as we were.

'I was thinking. Maybe this is it. Maybe this is the smallest place in the world. Just enough for all of us.'

'What happened?' says Margaret. 'Tell me about the day I asked you and what you said to me.'

'It was nothing much. You were on the floor with your head in the sideboard cupboard. I watched you climbing right inside. What you after? I said. I've lost Nancy in here, you said. The cupboard's too small to be lost in, I said. But she's so small, you said. I found the doll beside me on the settee. Here she is! I said. You ticked her off. Who said you could go off wandering all alone? You said. You came and sat on my knee and we looked at the open sideboard door and the dark cupboard. Could I have got lost in there? You said. Too small, I told you. You'd hardly get *in* it, never mind get lost in it. Look at the size of you and the size of that. We sat quiet for a while. The day was like this. Sun shining, blackbirds singing. After a while, you said, Where's the smallest place in the world? Then you said, What would we find sitting all safe inside?'

'What did you say?' says Margaret.

'Isn't it silly?' He smiles. 'I don't remember. But maybe this is it, this kitchen, and here we are, all sitting safe inside.'

Unchanging light, unchanging song; the lark, the blackbird, the children. The dust seethes and dances in the light. Catherine takes more toast from beneath the grill. We allow it to cool for a moment before putting the butter on.

'This one got lost,' says Mam. 'Went off wandering on her own, the smallest of us all. Who said you could do that, now?'

Barbara blushes and smiles.

'That was the smallest place,' she whispers. 'No room for anybody else but me in there.'

'I know,' says Mam. 'Oh, I know.'

'Thought you'd all forsaken me. Thought you'd all forget me.'

'I wasn't even here when you were here,' says Mary. 'But I still remember you. I still don't forget you.'

'I know that now,' says Barbara. 'But I thought I'd be alone for ever. Me so little and all of you so big. And so many of you, more of you even though I was gone. You'd have each other and the little memory of me would just get lost.'

'We never forgot,' says Dad. 'And if we didn't remember true, we just made bits up.'

Barbara laughs.

'Made bits up!'

'Yes. Truth and memories and dreams and bits made up.'

'Bits made up. But bits made up that kept me safe and real in all your hearts.'

We listen to the beating of our hearts.

Barbara says, 'When I began to understand, I used to come among you. I knew you knew I was there. I knew you knew I was always there.'

'Yes,' says Mam. 'We always knew.'

We smile at her. We listen to the blackbirds, to the children singing.

'Tell us about another day,' says Mary.

'Tell them about another day,' says Dad.

'We were at the beach,' says Mam. She touches Barbara. 'All of us but you. South Shields, another day like this, all burning bright. Dad and I sat by the bandstand and spread the blankets and towels on the grass. Mary and Margaret were on their hunkers at the sea's edge with their buckets, pouring sand into the sea and sea into the sand. Catherine knelt building a castle. The boys were right in, diving and swimming and yelling at the cold. We sat on the warm grass and leaned back on the warm bricks. Dad put a kettle on the primus. We saw the fret coming in. It was white and thick and so sudden. The horizon disappeared, then the great boat that was waiting to enter the Tyne, then the waves. And the fret came closer, until the boys were gone. You remember?'

'I remember,' says Dad. 'I ran down, and I called and called. I ran into the sea. The sea was icy cold and the air was icy cold. I stood there splashing, calling. You remember?'

'Yes,' says Colin. 'We heard you shouting and it was like you were a hundred miles away.'

'I stood up and watched,' says Mam. 'Dad in his soaking trousers, the girls behind him on the shore. I saw Dad running into the fret until he had disappeared, too.'

Dad laughs.

'Blundered into them, knocked them flying, tumbled into the sea myself. We came out icy cold and soaking wet.'

'Giggling and splashing,' says Mam. 'You all came up to me, to the bandstand, the tea, the sandwiches. Soon everybody wrapped in towels. You'll catch your deaths, I said. You will. You'll catch your deaths.'

We drink tea, nibble toast, try to remember.

'It was me that saw her,' says Catherine. 'The little girl standing in the fret, pale as the mist, knee-deep in the sea. I pointed. There! I said. There! We watched the fret, going back as quickly as it had come in. In the water, I said. There, in the fret. There. Peel your eyes. I ran down to the sea, pointing. There! The fret went back, the sea was empty, just water, little waves. Not a soul in there. Dreamed it night after night. Little girl in the water. The missing one, the one who seemed always to be somewhere in the fringes. Catch her in the corner of your eye, then turn your head and she'd be gone.'

We turn our eyes to Barbara. She turns her eyes to each of us, eyes shining like the sea, complexion pale as sea fret.

'I didn't make you up,' says Catherine.

'No,' says Barbara, and she reaches out and touches Catherine's cheek. 'And it doesn't matter exactly what's true and what's made up. I was always there. I am always there, despite my death.'

We are silent at the word, but we sigh together, those of us who are in life and those of us who are in death.

'What's death?' says Mary suddenly. Mary looks at Mam, at Dad, at Barbara. 'You all died. What's death?'

'Death is very big and very frightening,' says Barbara. 'Death is being all alone and waiting for others to come to you.'

'Death is separation,' says Dad. 'It's when you're torn away from those who have hardly known you, and who will have trouble in remembering you.' He touches Mary on the cheek. 'Like you and Margaret,' he says. 'You would always have difficulty in remembering me.'

'Death is knowing you're about to die,' says Mam. 'It's seeing the dead and seeing the living all at once. It's wanting not to die and not to live. It's wanting to stay with the last breath when the dead and the living are all around you, and touching you, and whispering. It's all right, Mam. Everything's all right. But there's no way of staying with the last breath. You have to die.'

'And then?' says Colin. 'What happens then?'

Barbara smiles.

'And then the dead get together and tell stories about the living, just as the living tell stories about the dead.'

'Yes,' says Dad. 'The dead begin with, Do you remember? Or Let me tell you about the time, or, There was once …'

We're silent again. We listen to the birds, the children singing outside.

Mam laughs.

'I sang that, ' she says. '*January, February, March, April* … Jumping the rope, running round to the line again. Time and again and time and again and time and again. There was once a little girl with lovely leaping legs …'

She hums the relentless tune and taps her toes on the floor.

'And anyway,' she says. 'As well as life and death, there's this.'

'What's this?' says Mary.

'The kitchen. Just the kitchen, I suppose.'

'The smallest place in the world,' says Dad. 'An impossible place. An impossible story. A kind of Heaven.'

'And what's Heaven?' says Colin.

'Maybe it's just this, an impossible afternoon when everyone is together all at once.'

We gaze out at the light, through the seething dust. The sun still hangs at the dead centre of the sky. The children and the blackbird sing. No one speaks. Nothing happens. We look at each other, touch each other.

'Tell us a story,' says Margaret.

'Tell us a story,' we say.

'There was once …' says Mam.

We look at her.

'Yes,' she whispers. 'Listen. This is true … Hm. There was once a little boy from Carlisle Street who lost his voice in the winter snow. You remember?'

'I remember,' says Dad.

'His name was Jack Law,' says Mam. 'He had seven sisters, a loving mammy and a loving daddy, and nowt but sacking tied around his feet …'

We listen to the truth, the memories, the bits made up. We gaze at each other. We eat warm buttered toast. We know that the sun will fall, that the children and the birds will be silent. We know that we will return to separate lives and separate deaths. We listen to the stories, that for an impossible afternoon hold back the coming dark.

Read, Think and Write

1. In 'Crossing Over', why did the girl volunteer to give up some of her time to help old people?

2. What jobs were on offer for her to choose from?

3. '... Togo was unruly and difficult to manage'.
   Find and write down other examples of how the writer describes the dog.

4. What does the girl think happened at the zebra crossing?

5. What does the phrase 'her courage evaporated' mean?

6. Why does the girl decide to go to Mrs Matthews' house?

7. How does the girl feel while she waits for Mrs Matthews to open the door?

8. How does the writer show that the girl is a ghost at the end of the story?

9. Look back through the story. What clues or hints does the writer give that the girl is a ghost?

10. Who is the ghost in 'The Kitchen'? How does the writer describe her appearance?

11. On what other occasion was she seen?

12. What does she say which shows how she feels about being dead?

13. Which other characters in the story speak about their experiences of death? What do they say about death?

14. Write a passage explaining which story you prefer. Use examples from the text to illustrate your choice.

Hint
Comment on the writer's style, the use of plot and the use of images.

Read and Analyse

1. In 'Crossing Over' the writer uses words with the prefixes <u>dis</u>, <u>un</u>, <u>mis</u>, <u>in</u> and <u>anti</u> when she describes Togo's behaviour. Find the words in the story and then use a dictionary to find other words with these prefixes.

   The prefixes are added to certain words to give them an opposite meaning. Make a list of words for each prefix. Use some of the words from your lists in sentences of your own.

2. 'The early evening walks weren't quite so bad, <u>because</u> there wasn't time to take him to the Common, <u>so</u> he stayed on the leash all the time.'

   Find other examples in the story where the writer has used conjunctions to develop the structure of a sentence.

   Write sentences of your own using the conjunctions <u>and</u>, <u>so</u>, <u>but</u> and <u>if</u>.

3. Use first-person narrative to write the story from Togo's point of view.

Read, Discuss and Act

1. Ghost stories are hard to believe. How well do you think 'Crossing Over' works as a ghost story? At what point in the story did you realise that the girl was a ghost? What ingredients would make a good ghost story?

2. David Almond has used real memories of death in his family when writing his story. Do you think that ghost stories are a good way of exploring ideas about death and dying? Do you think they could help people's fear of death?

3. The girl in 'Crossing Over' is unaware that she cannot be seen by anyone. In a small group of three or four, work out a scene to show a haunting that goes wrong, using the idea that at least one member of the group cannot be seen or heard by the others. Try to make your scene amusing.

The Big Sleep

by Raymond Chandler

Raymond Chandler developed the genre of the 'hard-boiled' detective through his character Philip Marlowe. This genre often uses first-person narrative to tell the story. The following extract is taken from the beginning of *The Big Sleep*, which was first published in 1939.

I

It was about eleven o'clock in the morning, mid October, with the sun not shining and a look of hard wet rain in the clearness of the foothills. I was wearing my powder-blue suit, with dark blue shirt, tie and display handkerchief, black brogues, black wool socks with dark blue clocks on them. I was neat, clean, shaved and sober, and I didn't care who knew it. I was everything the well-dressed private detective ought to be. I was calling on four million dollars.

The main hallway of the Sternwood place was two stories high. Over the entrance doors, which would have let in a troop of Indian elephants, there was a broad stained-glass panel showing a knight in dark armour rescuing a lady who was tied to a tree and didn't have any clothes on but some very long and convenient hair. The knight had pushed the vizor of his helmet back to be sociable, and he was fiddling with the knots on the ropes that tied the lady to the tree and not getting anywhere. I stood there and thought that if I lived in the house, I would sooner or later have to climb up there and help him. He didn't seem to be really trying.

There were French doors at the back of the hall, beyond them a wide sweep of emerald grass to a white garage, in front of which a slim dark young chauffeur in shiny black leggings was dusting a maroon Packard convertible. Beyond the garage were some decorative trees trimmed as carefully as poodle dogs. Beyond them a large greenhouse with a domed roof. Then more trees and beyond everything the solid, uneven, comfortable line of the foothills.

On the east side of the hall a free staircase, tile-paved, rose to a gallery with a wrought-iron railing and another piece of stained-glass romance. Large hard chairs with rounded red plush seats were backed into the vacant spaces of the wall round about. They didn't look as if anybody had ever sat in them. In the middle of the west wall there was a big empty fireplace with a brass screen in four hinged panels, and over the fireplace a marble mantel with cupids at the corners. Above the mantel there was a large oil portrait, and above the portrait two bullet-torn or moth-eaten cavalry pennants crossed in a glass frame. The portrait was a stiffly posed job of an officer in full regimentals of about the time of the Mexican War. The officer had a neat black imperial, black mustachios, hot hard coal-black eyes, and the general look of a man it would pay to get along with. I thought this might be General Sternwood's grandfather. It could hardly be the General himself, even though I had heard he was pretty far gone in years to have a couple of daughters still in the dangerous twenties.

I was still staring at the hot black eyes when a door opened far back under the stairs. It wasn't the butler coming back. It was a girl.

She was twenty or so, small and delicately put together, but she looked durable. She wore pale blue slacks and they looked well on her. She walked as if she were floating. Her hair was a fine tawny wave cut much shorter than the current fashion of pageboy tresses curled in at the bottom. Her eyes were slate-grey, and had almost no expression when they looked at me. She came over near me and smiled with her mouth and she had little sharp predatory teeth, as white as fresh orange pith and as shiny as porcelain. They glistened between her thin too taut lips. Her face lacked colour and didn't look too healthy.

'Tall, aren't you?' she said.

'I didn't mean to be.'

Her eyes rounded. She was puzzled. She was thinking. I could see, even on that short acquaintance, that thinking was always going to be a bother to her.

'Handsome too,' she said. 'And I bet you know it.'

I grunted.

'What's your name?'

'Reilly,' I said. 'Doghouse Reilly.'

'That's a funny name.' She bit her lip and turned her head a little and looked at me along her eyes. Then she lowered her lashes until they almost cuddled her cheeks and slowly raised them again, like a theatre curtain. I was to get to know that trick. That was supposed to make me roll over on my back with all four paws in the air.

'Are you a prizefighter?' she asked, when I didn't.

'Not exactly. I'm a sleuth.'

'A–a–' She tossed her head angrily, and the rich colour of it glistened in the rather dim light of the big hall. 'You're making fun of me.'

'Uh-uh.'

'What?'

'Get on with you,' I said. 'You heard me.'

'You didn't say anything. You're just a big tease.' She put a thumb up and bit it. It was a curiously shaped thumb, thin and narrow like an extra finger, with no curve in the first joint. She bit it and sucked it slowly, turning it around in her mouth like a baby with a comforter.

'You're awfully tall,' she said. Then she giggled with secret merriment. Then she turned her body slowly and lithely, without lifting her feet. Her hands dropped limp at her sides. She tilted herself towards me on her toes. She fell straight back into my arms. I had to catch her or let her crack her head on the tessellated floor. I caught her under her arms and she went rubber-legged on me instantly. I had to hold her close to hold her up. When her head was against my chest she screwed it around and giggled at me.

'You're cute,' she giggled. 'I'm cute too.'

I didn't say anything. So the butler chose that convenient moment to come back through the French doors and see me holding her.

It didn't seem to bother him. He was a tall thin silver man, sixty or close to it or a little past it. He had blue eyes as remote as eyes could be. His skin was smooth and bright and he moved like a man with very sound muscles. He walked slowly across the floor towards us and the girl jerked away from me. She flashed across the room to the foot of the stairs and went up them like a deer. She was gone before I could draw a long breath and let it out.

The butler said tonelessly: 'The General will see you now, Mr Marlowe.'

I pushed my lower jaw up off my chest and nodded at him. 'Who was that?'

'Miss Carmen Sternwood, sir.'

'You ought to wean her. She looks old enough.'

He looked at me with grave politeness and repeated what he had said.

II

We went out at the French doors and along a smooth red-flagged path that skirted the far side of the lawn from the garage. The boyish-looking chauffeur had a big black and chromium sedan out now and was dusting that. The path took us along to the side of the greenhouse and the butler opened a door for me and stood aside. It opened into a sort of vestibule that was about as warm as a slow oven. He came in after me, shut the outer door, opened an inner door and we went through that. Then it was really hot. The air was thick, wet, steamy and larded with the cloying smell of tropical orchids in bloom. The glass walls and roof were heavily misted and big drops of moisture splashed down on the plants. The light had an unreal greenish colour, like light filtered through an aquarium tank. The plants filled the place, a forest of them, with nasty meaty leaves and stalks like the newly washed fingers of dead men. They smelled as overpowering as boiling alcohol under a blanket.

The butler did his best to get me through without being smacked in the face by the sodden leaves, and after a while we came to a clearing in the middle of the jungle, under the domed roof. Here, in a space of hexagonal flags, an old red Turkish rug was laid down and on the rug was a wheel chair, and in the wheel chair an old and obviously dying man watched us come with black eyes from which all fire had died long ago, but which still had the coal-black directness of the eyes in the portrait that hung above the mantel in the hall. The rest of his face was a leaden mask, with the bloodless lips and the sharp nose and the sunken temples and the outward-turning ear-lobes of approaching dissolution. His long narrow body was wrapped – in that heat – in a travelling rug and a faded red bathrobe. His thin clawlike hands were folded loosely on the rug, purple-nailed. A few locks of dry white hair clung to his scalp, like wild flowers fighting for life on a bare rock.

The butler stood in front of him and said: 'This is Mr Marlowe, General.'

The old man didn't move or speak, or even nod. He just looked at me lifelessly. The butler pushed a damp wicker chair against the backs of my legs and I sat down. He took my hat with a deft scoop.

Then the old man dragged his voice up from the bottom of a well and said: 'Brandy, Norris. How do you like your brandy, sir?'

'Any way at all,' I said.

The butler went away among the abominable plants. The General spoke again, slowly, using his strength as carefully as an out-of-work showgirl uses her last good pair of stockings.

'I used to like mine with champagne. The champagne as cold as Valley Forge and about a third of a glass of brandy beneath it. You may take your coat off, sir. It's too hot in here for a man with blood in his veins.'

I stood up and peeled off my coat and got a handkerchief out and mopped my face and neck and the backs of my wrists. St Louis in August had nothing on that place. I sat down again and felt automatically for a cigarette and then stopped. The old man caught the gesture and smiled faintly.

'You may smoke, sir. I like the smell of tobacco.'

I lit the cigarette and blew a lungful at him and he sniffed at it like a terrier at a rat-hole. The faint smile pulled at the shadowed corners of his mouth.

Read, Think and Write

1. How does the narrator of the story describe himself?

2. What is his first impression of 'the Sternwood place'?

3. What impression does he give of Miss Carmen Sternwood?

4. The author has made the narrator someone who is very observant and notices detail, characteristics which are useful for a private detective. What does the narrator notice before entering the greenhouse which implies he has been observant since arriving at the house?

Hint
Check the beginning of the extract again.

5. Find and write down all the similes Marlowe uses to describe what he feels, sees and smells in the greenhouse.

6. In what way has the author made these similes appropriate for the character of the narrator?

7. Make notes on the butler's appearance and how he speaks and acts throughout the extract. What impression of him do you get from Marlowe's comments?

8. Look again at the extract and imagine it is being narrated by the butler. How would you write it from his point of view? How might he see Marlowe and the other characters – the chauffeur, Carmen Sternwood and his employer, the General.

    Marlowe's viewpoint makes the reader aware of his senses by the use of simile and adjectives. What style of language would be appropriate to use for the butler?

    Write the butler's account of the story up to the point where he leaves to get the brandy. Start with: 'I left Mr Marlowe waiting in the main hallway. When I returned …'

Read and Analyse

1. The use of pronouns is an indication that the story is being narrated in the first person. Starting at Chapter II, write out the first five sentences as though they were narrated in the third person, altering the pronouns as necessary.

2. List the adjectives used to describe General Sternwood's body. Use these adjectives to describe different nouns in sentences of your own.

3. The detective novels of the 1930s and 1940s were often used as a basis for film scripts. As well as writing books, Raymond Chandler worked as a Hollywood scriptwriter.

   Starting at the point where the butler introduces Marlowe to the General, change the format of the text into a film script.

Hint
Check the conventions of script writing before you start.

Read, Discuss and Act

1. When one of the characters tells the story we only get their point of view. How might this be a problem? Do you think Raymond Chandler wanted you to like the character who told the story? Would it make a difference to the story if the character was unpleasant and unlikeable? Can you think of other stories where the writer uses one of the characters to tell the story?

2. The detective genre is very popular. Can you name some other famous fictional detectives? What reasons could you give for this popularity?

3. Working in small groups, use a tape-recorder and present a performance of the extract from *The Big Sleep* as a radio play. You could use a narrator's voice to link the scenes. Consider tone of voice in your characterisations and the use of sound effects.

The Prisoner: Shattered Visage

by Dean Motter and Mark Askwith

During the 1960s the spy thriller became a very popular genre. The daring assignments of the James Bond novels, written by Ian Fleming, made espionage seem dangerous and heroic. In his graphic novel, Dean Motter has used the 1968 television show 'The Prisoner' as a starting point to develop a story which uses, but also questions, some of the conventions of that genre.

HELLO, SIR. YOU'VE A STACK OF MESSAGES AND A FOUR O'CLOCK MEETING WITH COLONEL J.

GET D. OPS DOWN HERE STRAIGHT AWAY!

YES, SIR.

MY POINT EXACTLY! I'VE BEEN CLEARED BACK TO THE CRIB. I THOUGHT THIS MIGHT HAVE SOMETHING TO DO WITH... UH... MY MARITAL DIFFICULTIES.

TAILED? YOU? WHY THE HELL WOULD I WANT TO WASTE MY BLOKES ON YOU?

HOW ARE THINGS BETWEEN YOU TWO?

FINE, FINE. SHE SENDS HER LOVE. WHY AM I A MARKED MAN?

I WOULDN'T KNOW. I HAVEN'T ASSIGNED ANYONE TO WATCH YOU.

WHO'S THAT THEN?

MARY POPPINS?!

I BELIEVE THAT'S SPECIAL OP. LAKE. --AND I'M ONE OF THE DOGS HE WALKS.

I MUST REPRIMAND HIM FOR BEING SPOTTED, YES, IT'S LAKE ALRIGHT, BUT I LOANED HIM TO THE GODS LAST WEEK.

103

105

NO, SIR.

I AM WORRIED BY WHAT APPEARS TO BE A NARROWING IN SCOPE OF MY DEPARTMENT'S MANDATE. IN MY VIEW, *EXCAVATIONS*, ALWAYS A JUNIOR OFFICE, RISKS EXTINCTION IF CURRENT POLITICS PREVAIL.

YES?

REQUESTS FOR EXTRA STAFF: DENIED.

REQUESTS FOR EXTRA FUNDING: DEFERRED.

PETITION FOR SPECIAL AGENT: REJECTED.

PETITION FOR INTER-DEPARTMENTAL ASSISTANCE: DENIED.

YOUR DEPARTMENT HAS OPERATED AT CERTAIN STAFF AND BUDGET LEVELS FOR DECADES. NOW, YOUR ENTHUSIASM IS COMMENDABLE, BUT SOME MIGHT SEE YOUR REQUESTS...

...AS LITTLE MORE THAN ...EMPIRE BUILDING.

MY REQUESTS ARE LEGITIMATE, SIR. ON MONDAY, THE MAN YOU CALL *NUMBER TWO* WILL BE RELEASED FROM PRISON AFTER TWENTY YEARS. IN HIS ORIGINAL MANUSCRIPT HE MADE CERTAIN ALLEGATIONS.

I'VE TOLD YOU THAT, DESPITE OUR CONCESSIONS, HE PLANS TO AVENGE HIMSELF ON THOSE RESPONSIBLE FOR HIS INCARCERATION. ALL I WANT IS A SPECIAL AGENT TO RUN INTERFERENCE.

DO YOU REALLY THINK *NUMBER TWO* IS A THREAT? HE WAS, AFTER ALL, QUITE HANDSOMELY COMPENSATED.

YES, SIR. TO THE POINT THAT I AM PREPARED TO BACK MY CONCERN...

...WITH MY RESIGNATION.

DON'T BE A FOOL, THOMAS.

YOU ARE NOT THE QUITTING TYPE.

NO, YOU ARE A CLEVER, RESOURCEFUL MAN.

YOU'LL FIND SOME ELEGANT SOLUTION TO THIS DILEMMA.

WHERE?

I CANNOT OFFICIALLY CONDONE ANY DEPARTMENTAL ACTION TO AID YOU.

GOOD DAY, THOMAS.

Read, Think and Write

1. What does the phrase 'shattered visage' mean?

2. What is the name of the Director of Operations?

3. 'You've got me tailed … ' Who is following Thomas?

4. Why does the Director of Operations know nothing about Thomas being 'tailed'?

5. How do the writer and illustrator show that the older man, whom Thomas visits, is a figure of authority?

6. What do we learn about the 'lovely wife'?

7. What do we learn about 'Number Two'?

8. Why does Thomas think Number Two is a threat?

9. Why does the older man disagree with him?

10. Use information in the illustrations and written text to write a character sketch of Thomas. Use your imagination to fill in missing detail.

> **His appearance and self-image**
> Would he care what sort of car he drove?
>
> **His home life**
> Is he happily married?
>
> **Is he ambitious?**
> He works in the 'Excavations Department'. What do you think he does?

11. Change the illustrated form of the first page of the extract into a written text form. Your text should be in four paragraphs, based on the ideas in the four illustrations. Use simple sentences and complex sentences in each paragraph and remember to use the conventions of speech in your final paragraph.

Read and Analyse

1. In your own words write down the meaning of the following phrases. Use a dictionary to check unfamiliar words. Refer back to the text and read the phrases in context to understand their meaning.

'a narrowing in scope of my department's mandate'
'requests for extra funding deferred'
'your enthusiasm is commendable'
'my requests are legitimate'
'he made certain allegations'
'despite our concessions'
'to avenge himself on those responsible for his incarceration'
'he was ... handsomely compensated'

2. Write a simple sentence and a complex sentence to describe each of the following characters shown or mentioned in the extract:

Thomas' wife   Number Two
The Director of Operations   The Colonel

Read, Discuss and Act

1. How might political and technological changes alter the plots of spy stories?

2. Do you think the graphic novel is a good form for the genre? What other genres do you think could use the form of the graphic novel successfully?

3. In pairs, role-play a scene where an agent is discussing a case with his/her Director of Operations. A possible structure for the scene could be:

The agent reports the progress of the mission he/she has been working on. The Director of Operations gives the agent new orders for the mission.

You might try to develop the scene to a point where it becomes clear that one of the characters is a double agent and therefore becomes a threat to the other one.

Oliver Twist and Great Expectations

by Charles Dickens

Charles Dickens was a writer who left us with a distinctive impression of life in the nineteenth century. Many of his novels started as monthly or weekly episodes of stories in magazines. *Oliver Twist* was serialised monthly in 1837–39 and *Great Expectations* was serialised weekly in 1860–61. In the search for information about social behaviour, history books can provide factual material but novels can also give a stylistic impression of life at that time. Dickens' plots and characters were fictional but the settings and conditions he describes reflect what life was like for some people in the nineteenth century.

Oliver Twist

Chapter 1
Treats of the place where Oliver Twist was born; and of the circumstances attending his birth

Among other public buildings in a certain town, which for many reasons it will be prudent to refrain from mentioning, and to which I will assign no fictitious name, there is one anciently common to most towns, great or small: to wit, a workhouse; and in this workhouse was born: on a day and date which I need not trouble myself to repeat, inasmuch as it can be of no possible consequence to the reader, in this stage of the business at all events: the item of mortality whose name is prefixed to the head of this chapter.

For a long time after it was ushered into this world of sorrow and trouble, by the parish surgeon, it remained a matter of considerable doubt whether the child would survive to bear any name at all; in which case it is somewhat more than probable that these memoirs would never have appeared; or, if they had, that being comprised within a couple of pages, they would have possessed the inestimable merit of being the most concise and faithful specimen of biography, extant in the literature of any age or country.

Although I am not disposed to maintain that the being born in a workhouse, is in itself the most fortunate and enviable circumstance that can possibly befall a human being, I do mean to say that in this particular instance, it was the best thing for Oliver Twist that could by possibility have occurred. The fact is, that there was considerable difficulty in inducing Oliver to take upon himself the office of respiration, – a troublesome practice, but one which custom has rendered necessary to our easy existence; and for some time he lay gasping on a little flock mattress, rather unequally poised between this world and the next: the balance being decidedly in favour of the latter. Now, if, during this brief period, Oliver had been surrounded by careful grandmothers, anxious aunts, experienced nurses, and doctors of profound wisdom, he would most inevitably and indubitably have been killed in no time. There being nobody by, however, but a pauper old woman, who was rendered rather misty by an unwonted allowance of beer; and a parish surgeon who did such matters by contract; Oliver and Nature fought out the point between them. The result was, that, after a few struggles, Oliver breathed, sneezed, and proceeded to advertise to the inmates of the workhouse the fact of a new burden having been imposed upon the parish, by setting up as loud as cry as could reasonably have been expected from a male infant who had not been possessed of that very useful appendage, a voice, for a much longer space of time than three minutes and a quarter.

As Oliver gave this first proof of the free and proper action of his lungs, the patchwork coverlet which was carelessly flung over the iron bedstead, rustled; the pale face of a young woman was raised feebly from the pillow; and a faint voice imperfectly articulated the words, 'Let me see the child, and die.'

The surgeon had been sitting with his face turned towards the fire: giving the palms of his hands a warm and a rub alternately. As the young woman spoke, he rose, and advancing to the bed's head, said, with more kindness than might have been expected of him:

'Oh, you must not talk about dying yet.'

'Lor bless her dear heart, no!' interposed the nurse, hastily depositing in her pocket a green glass bottle, the contents of which she had been tasting in a corner with evident satisfaction. 'Lor bless her dear heart, when she has lived as long as I have, sir, and had thirteen children of her own, and all on 'em dead except two, and them in the wurkus with me, she'll know better than to take on in that way, bless her dear heart! Think what it is to be a mother, there's a dear young lamb, do.'

Apparently this consolatory perspective of a mother's prospects, failed in producing its due effect. The patient shook her head, and stretched out her hand towards the child.

The surgeon deposited it in her arms. She imprinted her cold white lips passionately on its forehead; passed her hands over her face; gazed wildly round; shuddered; fell back – and died. They chafed her breast, hands, and temples; but the blood had stopped for ever. They talked of hope and comfort. They had been strangers too long.

'It's all over, Mrs. Thingummy!' said the surgeon at last.

'Ah, poor dear, so it is!' said the nurse, picking up the cork of the green bottle which had fallen out on the pillow as she stooped to take up the child. 'Poor dear!'

'You needn't mind sending up to me, if the child cries, nurse,' said the surgeon, putting on his gloves with great deliberation. 'It's very likely it *will* be troublesome. Give it a little gruel if it is.' He put on his hat, and, pausing by the bedside on his way to the door, added 'She was a good-looking girl, too; where did she come from?'

'She was brought here last night,' replied the old woman, 'by the overseer's order. She was found lying in the street. She had walked some distance, for her shoes were worn to pieces; but where she came from, or where she was going to, nobody knows.'

The surgeon leaned over the body, and raised the left hand. 'The old story,' he said, shaking his head: 'no wedding-ring, I see. Ah! Good night!'

Great Expectations

Chapter 1

My father's family name being Pirrip, and my christian name Philip, my infant tongue could make of both names nothing longer or more explicit than Pip. So, I called myself Pip, and came to be called Pip.

I give Pirrip as my father's family name, on the authority of his tombstone and my sister – Mrs. Joe Gargery, who married the blacksmith. As I never saw my father or my mother, and never saw any likeness of either of them (for their days were long before the days of photographs), my first fancies regarding what they were like, were unreasonably derived from their tombstones. The shape of the letters on my father's, gave me an odd idea that he was a square, stout, dark man, with curly black hair. From the character and turn of the inscription, "Also Georgiana Wife of the Above," I drew a childish conclusion that my mother was freckled and sickly. To five little stone lozenges, each about a foot and a half long, which were arranged in a neat row beside their grave, and were sacred to the memory of five little brothers of mine – who gave up trying to get a living, exceedingly early in that universal struggle – I am indebted for a belief I religiously entertained that they had all been born on their backs with their hands in their trousers-pockets, and had never taken them out in this state of existence.

Ours was the marsh country, down by the river, within, as the river wound, twenty miles of the sea. My first most vivid and broad impression of the identity of things, seems to me to have been gained on a memorable raw afternoon towards evening. At such a time I found out for certain, that this bleak place overgrown with nettles was the churchyard; and that Philip Pirrip, late of this parish, and also Georgiana wife of the above, were dead and buried; and that Alexander, Bartholomew, Abraham, Tobias, and Roger, infant children of the aforesaid, were also dead and buried; and that the dark flat wilderness beyond the churchyard, intersected with dykes and mounds and gates, with scattered cattle feeding on it, was the marshes; and that the low leaden line beyond, was the river; and that the distant savage lair from which the wind was rushing, was the sea; and that the small bundle of shivers growing afraid of it all and beginning to cry, was Pip.

"Hold your noise!" cried a terrible voice, as a man started up from among the graves at the side of the church porch. "Keep still, you little devil, or I'll cut your throat!"

A fearful man, all in coarse grey, with a great iron on his leg. A man with no hat, and with broken shoes, and with an old rag tied round his head. A man who had been soaked in water, and smothered in mud, and lamed by stones, and cut by flints, and stung by nettles, and torn by briars; who limped, and shivered, and glared and growled; and whose teeth chattered in his head as he seized me by the chin.

"O! Don't cut my throat, sir," I pleaded in terror. "Pray don't do it, sir."

"Tell us your name!" said the man. "Quick!"

"Pip, sir."

"Once more," said the man, staring at me. "Give it mouth!"

"Pip. Pip, sir!"

"Show us where you live," said the man. "Pint out the place!"

I pointed to where our village lay, on the flat in-shore among the alder-trees and pollards, a mile or more from the church.

The man, after looking at me for a moment, turned me upside-down and emptied my pockets. There was nothing in them but a piece of bread. When the church came to itself – for he was so sudden and strong that he made it go head over heels before me, and I saw the steeple under my feet – when the church came to itself, I say, I was seated on a high tombstone, trembling, while he ate the bread ravenously.

1. Where was Oliver Twist born?

2. What does the phrase 'the office of respiration' mean?

3. Who would have 'indubitably' killed Oliver had they been around?

4. Who was around at the birth?

5. What is the meaning of 'Oliver and Nature fought out the point between them'?

6. Why was the old woman not much help to Oliver?

7. How did they know Oliver was alive?

8. Where was the mother and what did she do when she was handed the baby?

9. Why is the child in *Great Expectations* called Pip?

10. Where are his parents?

11. What time of day is it when he is in the churchyard?

12. How does Dickens describe Pip just before the stranger appears?

13. Look at the paragraph in *Great Expectations* that describes the setting. Write down the words and phrases Dickens uses to describe the following features of the landscape: the churchyard; the marshes; the river; the sea.

14. Write down some words and phrases that would describe the following possible settings for a nineteenth-century novel in a bleak and depressing way: a factory; town streets; a cottage in a village; a country lane.

Read and Analyse

1. Find the paragraph which describes the stranger in *Great Expectations*. Look carefully at the third sentence. Dickens uses verbs rather than adjectives to describe him. Write down the verbs he uses.

2. How does Dickens make the dialogue urgent and threatening in *Great Expectations*?

Hint
Look at sentence structure and use of punctuation.

3. Write down the meaning of these words:

pauper	burden	inevitable
rendered	appendage	indubitable

'Indubitable' and 'inevitable' have been used as adverbs in the extract from *Oliver Twist* by the addition of the suffix 'ly'. Look through the extract and find other adverbs with the 'ly' suffix.

4. Both Oliver and Pip are orphans. How do the extracts show this?

5. Write the first episode of a story for a nineteenth-century magazine in the style of Charles Dickens. Refer to the extracts for the sort of vocabulary and sentence structure that Dickens uses. Have an orphan as the central character. The episode could explain why and how the child becomes orphaned and what happens to him/her. Leave the story on a 'cliffhanger' to make people want to read the next episode.

Read, Discuss and Act

1. In the nineteenth century childhood was a difficult time, according to many of Dickens' novels. What evidence is there in the extracts that life was hard? What things have been important to you in your childhood? If you were able to choose what period of time you were born into, when would you choose and why?

2. In pairs, act out the scene between Pip and the threatening stranger. As a contrast, develop your own scene where an adult is showing concern and care for a child.

The Prelude

by William Wordsworth

Happy calf

by Ted Hughes

William Wordsworth wrote 'The Prelude' between 1798 and 1805. It is a long autobiographical poem. This short extract is taken from the childhood and schooltime section of Book1. Wordsworth spent this part of his life in the Lake District and his poetry reflects a love and understanding of the countryside which surrounded him. Ted Hughes' poem 'Happy calf' is from a set of poems entitled *Moortown*, which is 'a kind of verse journal of his experiences farming in Devon'. It was published in 1979. The two poems are separated by a wide expanse of time but both convey vivid images of the countryside.

Extract from The Prelude

Nor less in springtime when on southern banks
The shining sun had from his knot of leaves
Decoy'd the primrose flower, and when the Vales
And woods were warm, was I a plunderer then
In the high places, on the lonesome peaks
Where'er, among the mountains and the winds,
The Mother Bird had built her lodge. Though mean
My object, and inglorious, yet the end
Was not ignoble. Oh! when I have hung
Above the raven's nest, by knots of grass
And half-inch fissures in the slippery rock
But ill sustain'd, and almost, as it seem'd

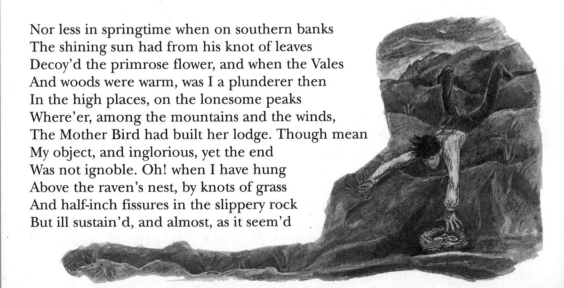

Suspended by the blast which blew amain,
Shouldering the naked crag; Oh! at that time;
While on the perilous ridge I hung alone,
With what strange utterance did the loud dry wind
Blow through my ears! the sky seem'd not a sky
Of earth, and with what motion mov'd the clouds!

Happy calf

Mother is worried, her low, short moos
Question what's going on. But her calf
Is quite happy, resting on his elbows,
With his wrists folded under, and his precious hind legs
Brought up beside him, his little hooves
Of hardly-used yellow-soled black.
She looms up, to reassure him with heavy lickings.
He wishes she'd go away. He's meditating
Black as a mole and as velvety,
With a white face-mask, and a pink parting,
With black tear-patches, but long
Glamorous white eyelashes. A mild narrowing
Of his eyes, as he lies, testing each breath
For its peculiar flavour of being alive.
Such a pink muzzle, but a black dap
Where he just touched his mother's blackness
With a tentative sniff. He is all quiet
While his mother worries to and fro, grazes a little,
Then looks back, a shapely mass
Against the South sky and the low frieze of hills,
And moos questioning warning. He just stays,
Head slightly tilted, in the mild illness
Of being quite contented, and patient
With all the busyness inside him, the growing
Getting under way. The wind from the North
Marching the high silvery floor of clouds
Trembles the grass-stalks near him. His head wobbles
Infinitesimally in the pulse of his life.
A buttercup leans on his velvet hip.
He folds his head back little by breathed little
Till it rests on his shoulder, his nose on his ankle,
And he sleeps. Only his ears stay awake.

117

Read, Think and Write

1. Wordsworth is 'bird-nesting' or stealing birds' eggs. What words in the poem show that he knows this is wrong and he is ashamed now for having done this in his youth?

2. What phrases in the poem show that what he is doing is dangerous?

3. Write down three things referred to in the poem that show what season it is.

4. What words or phrases show that Wordsworth is in an upland region?

5. What words or phrases in the poem reveal Wordsworth's awareness of the mystery and power of life?

6. The calf in Ted Hughes' poem seems to be aware of the intensity and mystery of life. Which line or lines do you think indicate this?

7. Which lines in 'Happy calf' describe the setting and the weather?

8. Write down the words or phrases that show the mother's concern for her calf.

9. Write down the words or phrases that show the calf's feelings.

10. Write a description of the calf's appearance.

11. Which poem do you prefer? Give reasons for your preference.

12. Write a comparison of the two poems, referring to the similarities and differences in both form and content.

Hint
Think about poetic devices. Do the poems use rhyme, assonance, alliteration, metaphor and simile, etc.?
Try a syllable count on the lines.

Use a dictionary to find and write down the definitions of these words:

> decoy   inglorious   fissures   perilous
> plunderer   ignoble   sustained   utterance

Which of the words above have a prefix which if removed would give an opposite meaning?

2. Write down a list of nouns from the extract from 'The Prelude' that name features in the landscape: e.g. woods, peaks.

Take each word in your list and give it a winter image: e.g. snow-flurried woods, mirror-iced peaks.

Use the list again to create summer images. Try to use alliteration with some of them: e.g. sun-soaked woods, tall toasted peaks.

3. Reread the description of the calf in Ted Hughes' poem. Notice that the poet uses simile. Make a list of six animals you might find in the country: e.g. a hedgehog. Write a descriptive image for each animal: e.g. 'a sharp-suited little fellow with a nose that nudged the leaves like an energetic road sweeper's brush'.

1. In the poem, Wordsworth is hunting for birds' eggs. The countryside has always been a focus for hunting. What are your views on the subject?

Is the calf lucky to be enjoying the grass and the buttercups leaning on 'his velvet hip'? Consumers' demand for veal may mean that its life will be short. What sort of quality of life should animals have? There have been problems with animal diseases recently; is organic farming the answer?

What sort of future do you see for the countryside?

2. In small groups, prepare and present a reading of one of the poems as either an introduction or a conclusion to a presentation of your views on the future of the countryside.

Top Girls

by Caryl Churchill

The Importance of Being Earnest

by Oscar Wilde

Top Girls was first performed in 1982, nearly ninety years after the first performance of *The Importance of Being Earnest*. Both writers have used the play form to comment on aspects of the society they were living in at the time. When Caryl Churchill wrote *Top Girls*, Margaret Thatcher had just become Prime Minister. The play reflects the changes in the way women viewed their roles in society, changes which had developed throughout the 1970s. Oscar Wilde's play satirises the behaviour and beliefs of the aristocracy and upper-class Victorian society within which he lived and worked.

Top Girls

Act Two
Scene One

Employment Agency. MARLENE and JEANINE.

MARLENE. Right Jeanine, you are Jeanine aren't you? Let's have a look. Os and As. / No As, all those Os you probably

JEANINE. Six Os.

MARLENE. could have got an A. / Speeds, not brilliant, not too bad.

JEANINE. I wanted to go to work.

MARLENE. Well, Jeanine, what's your present job like?

JEANINE. I'm a secretary.

MARLENE. Secretary or typist?

JEANINE. I did start as a typist but the last six months I've been a secretary.

MARLENE. To?

JEANINE. To three of them really, they share me. There's Mr Ashford, he's the office manager, and Mr Philby / is sales, and –

MARLENE. Quite a small place?

JEANINE. A bit small.

MARLENE. Friendly?

JEANINE. Oh it's friendly enough.

MARLENE. Prospects?

JEANINE. I don't think so, that's the trouble. Miss Lewis is secretary to the managing director and she's been there forever, and Mrs Bradford / is –

MARLENE. So you want a job with better prospects?

JEANINE. I want a change.

MARLENE. So you'll take anything comparable?

JEANINE. No, I do want prospects. I want more money.

MARLENE. You're getting – ?

JEANINE. Hundred.

MARLENE. It's not bad you know. You're what? Twenty?

JEANINE. I'm saving to get married.

MARLENE. Does that mean you don't want a long-term job, Jeanine?

JEANINE. I might do.

MARLENE. Because where do the prospects come in? No kids for a bit?

JEANINE. Oh no, not kids, not yet.

MARLENE. So you won't tell them you're getting married?

JEANINE. Had I better not?

MARLENE. It would probably help.

JEANINE. I'm not wearing a ring. We thought we wouldn't spend on a ring.

MARLENE. Saves taking it off.

JEANINE. I wouldn't take it off.

MARLENE. There's no need to mention it when you go for an interview. / Now Jeanine do you have a feel for any particular

JEANINE. But what if they ask?

MARLENE. kind of company?

JEANINE. I thought advertising.

MARLENE. People often do think advertising. I have got a few vacancies but I think they're looking for something glossier.

JEANINE. You mean how I dress? / I can dress different. I

MARLENE. I mean experience.

JEANINE. dress like this on purpose for where I am now.

MARLENE. I have a marketing department here of a knitwear manufacturer. / Marketing is near enough advertising. Secretary

JEANINE. Knitwear?

MARLENE. to the marketing manager, he's thirty-five, married, I've sent him a girl before and she was happy, left to have a baby, you won't want to mention marriage there. He's very fair I think, good at his job, you won't have to nurse him along. Hundred and ten, so that's better than you're doing now.

JEANINE. I don't know.

MARLENE. I've a fairly small concern here, father and two sons, you'd have more say potentially, secretarial and reception duties, only a hundred but the job's going to grow with the concern and then you'll be in at the top with new girls coming in underneath you.

JEANINE. What is it they do?

MARLENE. Lampshades. / This would be my first choice for you.

JEANINE. Just lampshades?

MARLENE. There's plenty of different kinds of lampshade. So we'll send you there, shall we, and the knitwear second choice. Are you free to go for an interview any day they call you?

JEANINE. I'd like to travel.

MARLENE. We don't have any foreign clients. You'd have to go elsewhere.

JEANINE. Yes I know. I don't really … I just mean …

MARLENE. Does your fiancé want to travel?

JEANINE. I'd like a job where I was here in London and with him and everything but now and then – I expect it's silly. Are there jobs like that?

MARLENE. There's personal assistant to a top executive in a multinational. If that's the idea you need to be planning ahead. Is that where you want to be in ten years?

JEANINE. I might not be alive in ten years.

MARLENE. Yes but you will be. You'll have children.

JEANINE. I can't think about ten years.

MARLENE. You haven't got the speeds anyway. So I'll send you to these two shall I? You haven't been to any other agency? Just so we don't get crossed wires. Now Jeanine I want you to get one of these jobs, all right? If I send you that means I'm putting myself on the line for you. Your presentation's OK, you look fine, just be confident and go in there convinced that this is the best job for you and you're the best person for the job. If you don't believe it they won't believe it.

JEANINE. Do you believe it?

MARLENE. I think you could make me believe it if you put your mind to it.

JEANINE. Yes, all right.

The Importance of Being Earnest

LADY BRACKNELL: Mr Worthing! Rise, sir, from this semi-recumbent posture. It is most indecorous.

GWENDOLEN: Mamma! [*He tries to rise; she restrains him.*] I must beg you to retire. This is no place for you. Besides, Mr Worthing has not quite finished yet.

LADY BRACKNELL: Finished what, may I ask?

GWENDOLEN: I am engaged to Mr Worthing, mamma. [*They rise together.*]

LADY BRACKNELL: Pardon me, you are not engaged to anyone. When you do become engaged to some one, I, or your father, should his health permit him, will inform you of the fact. An engagement should come on a young girl as a surprise, pleasant or unpleasant, as the case my be. It is hardly a matter that she could be allowed to arrange for herself. … And now I have a few questions to put to you, Mr Worthing. While I am making these inquiries, you, Gwendolen, will wait for me below in the carriage.

GWENDOLEN [*reproachfully*]: Mamma!

LADY BRACKNELL: In the carriage, Gwendolen! [GWENDOLEN *goes to the door. She and* JACK *blow kisses to each other behind* LADY BRACKNELL'S *back.* LADY BRACKNELL *looks vaguely about as if she could not understand what the noise was. Finally turns round.*] Gwendolen, the carriage!

GWENDOLEN: Yes, mamma. [*Goes out, looking back at* JACK.]

LADY BRACKNELL [*sitting down*]: You can take a seat, Mr Worthing.

[*Looks in her pocket for note-book and pencil.*]

JACK: Thank you, Lady Bracknell, I prefer standing.

LADY BRACKNELL [*pencil and note-book in hand*]: I feel bound to tell you that you are not down on my list of eligible young men, although I have the same list as the dear Duchess of Bolton has. We work together, in fact. However, I am quite ready to enter your name, should your answers be what a really affectionate mother requires. Do you smoke?

JACK: Well, yes, I must admit I smoke.

LADY BRACKNELL: I am glad to hear it. A man should always have an occupation of some kind. There are far too many idle men in London as it is. How old are you?

JACK: Twenty-nine.

LADY BRACKNELL: A very good age to be married at. I have always been of opinion that a man who desires to get married should know either everything or nothing. Which do you know?

JACK [*after some hesitation*]: I know nothing, Lady Bracknell.

LADY BRACKNELL: I am please to hear it. I do not approve of anything that tampers with natural ignorance. Ignorance is like a delicate exotic fruit;

touch it and the bloom is gone. The whole theory of modern education is radically unsound. Fortunately in England, at any rate, education produces no effect whatsoever. If it did, it would prove a serious danger to the upper classes, and probably lead to acts of violence in Grosvenor Square. What is your income?

JACK: Between seven and eight thousand a year.

LADY BRACKNELL [*makes a note in her book*]: In land, or in investments?

JACK: In investments, chiefly.

LADY BRACKNELL: That is satisfactory. What between the duties expected of one during one's lifetime, and the duties exacted from one after one's death, land has ceased to be either a profit or a pleasure. It gives one position, and prevents one from keeping it up. That's all that can be said about land.

JACK: I have a country house with some land, of course, attached to it, about fifteen hundred acres, I believe: but I don't depend on that for my real income. In fact, as far as I can make out, the poachers are the only people who make anything out of it.

LADY BRACKNELL: A country house! How many bedrooms? Well, that point can be cleared up afterwards. You have a town house, I hope? A girl with a simple, unspoiled nature, like Gwendolen, could hardly be expected to reside in the country.

JACK: Well, I own a house in Belgrave Square, but it is let by the year to Lady Bloxham. Of course, I can get it back whenever I like, at six months' notice.

LADY BRACKNELL: Lady Bloxham? I don't know her.

JACK: Oh, she goes about very little. She is a lady considerably advanced in years.

LADY BRACKNELL: Ah, nowadays that is no guarantee of respectability of character. What number in Belgrave Square?

JACK: 149.

LADY BRACKNELL [*shaking her head*]: The unfashionable side. I thought there was something. However, that could easily be altered.

JACK: Do you mean the fashion, or the side?

LADY BRACKNELL [*sternly*]: Both, if necessary, I presume. What are your politics?

JACK: Well, I am afraid I really have none. I am a Liberal Unionist.

LADY BRACKNELL: Oh, they count as Tories. They dine with us. Or come in the evening, at any rate. Now to minor matters. Are your parents living?

JACK: I have lost both my parents.

LADY BRACKNELL: To lose one parent, Mr Worthing, may be regarded as a misfortune; to lose both looks like carelessness. Who was your father? He was evidently a man of some wealth. Was he born in what the Radical papers call the purple of commerce, or did he rise from the ranks of the aristocracy?

JACK: I am afraid I really don't know. The fact is, Lady Bracknell, I said I had lost my parents. It would be nearer the truth to say that my parents seem to have lost me. … I don't actually know who I am by birth. I was … well, I was found.

LADY BRACKNELL: Found!

JACK: The late Mr Thomas Cardew, an old gentleman of a very charitable and kindly disposition, found me, and gave me the name of Worthing, because he happened to have a first-class ticket for Worthing in his pocket at the time. Worthing is a place in Sussex. It is a seaside resort.

LADY BRACKNELL: Where did the charitable gentleman who had a first-class ticket for this seaside resort find you?

JACK [*gravely*]: In a hand-bag.

LADY BRACKNELL: A hand-bag?

JACK [*very seriously*]: Yes, Lady Bracknell. I was in a hand-bag – a somewhat large, black leather hand-bag, with handles to it – an ordinary hand-bag in fact.

LADY BRACKNELL: In what locality did this Mr James, or Thomas, Cardew come across this ordinary hand-bag?

JACK: In the cloak-room at Victoria Station. It was given to him in mistake for his own.

LADY BRACKNELL: The cloak-room at Victoria Station?

JACK: Yes. The Brighton line.

LADY BRACKNELL: The line is immaterial. Mr Worthing, I confess I feel somewhat bewildered by what you have just told me. To be born, or at any rate bred, in a hand-bag, whether it had handles or not, seems to me to display a contempt for the ordinary decencies of family life that reminds one of the worst excesses of the French Revolution. And I presume you know what that unfortunate movement led to? As for the particular locality in which the hand-bag was found, a cloak-room at a railway station might serve to conceal a social indiscretion – has probably, indeed, been used for that purpose before now – but it could hardly be regarded as an assured basis for a recognized position in good society.

JACK: May I ask you then what you would advise me to do? I need hardly say I would do anything in the world to ensure Gwendolen's happiness.

LADY BRACKNELL: I would strongly advise you, Mr Worthing, to try and acquire some relations as soon as possible, and to make a definite effort to produce at any rate one parent, of either sex, before the season is quite over.

JACK: Well, I don't see how I could possibly manage to do that. I can produce the hand-bag at any moment. It is in my dressing-room at home. I really think that should satisfy you, Lady Bracknell.

LADY BRACKNELL: Me, sir! What has it to do with me? You can hardly imagine that I and Lord Bracknell would dream of allowing our only daughter – a girl brought up with the utmost care – to marry into a cloak-room, and form an alliance with a parcel. Good morning, Mr Worthing!

[LADY BRACKNELL *sweeps out in majestic indignation.*]

1. Both extracts take the form of an interview between the two characters. What sort of interview is taking place in *Top Girls* and which character is controlling it?

2. How does Jeanine describe her present job to Marlene?

3. What evidence does the writer give to show that Marlene does not think Jeanine has the potential to improve her job prospects very much?

4. What is Marlene's view of marriage and work?

5. What advice does Marlene give Jeanine at the end of the interview?

6. What sort of interview is taking place in *The Importance of Being Earnest* and which character is controlling it?

7. What is Lady Bracknell's view of engagement and marriage?

8. Name four things that Lady Bracknell finds pleasing about Jack, and give the reasons why she is pleased.

9. Where was Jack found and how did he get his surname?

10. What advice does Lady Bracknell give Jack at the end of their interview?

11. Write a paragraph explaining Lady Bracknell's views on education and the ownership of land.

12. Caryl Churchill has given very few stage directions for the scene in *Top Girls*. Imagine you are the director of this play. Write a short passage explaining how you would set the stage. What props would you use to indicate that the set was an employment agency? What advice would you give the actors to help them develop the performance of the characters they are playing?

Read and Analyse

1. In your own words write down the meaning of the following words and phrases:

   - this semi-recumbent posture
   - indecorous   • eligible   • kindly disposition
   - to conceal a social indiscretion
   - a contempt for the ordinary decencies of family life

   Use a dictionary and refer back to the extract from *The Importance of Being Earnest* to read the words in context.

2. People often interrupt or talk over each other in a conversation. Look at the opening lines of the *Top Girls* extract. How has Caryl Churchill tried to alert the actors to this effect in the text?

   Write a similar scene from a play entitled *Top Boys*. The scene could take place in an employment agency or it could have a different setting, such as a music studio or an army recruitment centre. Use the conventions of a playscript to show what the male characters are like and how they would act.

   Hint
   You could use Caryl Churchill's method of indicating interruption or talking over each other.

Read, Discuss and Act

1. In what ways are these extracts similar? In what ways are they different? Which extract do you prefer and why?

2. Oscar Wilde's play is a satirical comedy. What does 'satirical' mean? Is this a good form for commenting on social behaviour? Can you think of any modern satirical comedies?

3. In pairs or threes (depending on which extract is used), choose one of the extracts and give a reading or a performance of it.

4. In pairs, act out your own interview scene. Try to make your characters' dialogue and actions critical of some aspect of social behaviour, e.g. sexism, ageism.

Acknowledgements

The publishers would like to thank the following copyright holders for permission to reproduce the extracts used in this book:

Harry Potter and the Chamber of Secrets. Copyright © J. K. Rowling 1998.
The Dark is Rising by Susan Cooper, published by Chatto & Windus. Used by permission of The Random House Group Limited.
Holes by Louis Sachar. Used by permission of Bloomsbury Publishing plc.
Forever X by Geraldine McCaughrean. Used by permission of Oxford University Press.
Abomination by Robert Swindells, published by Doubleday, a division of Transworld Publishers. All rights reserved. © Robert Swindells 1998.
'Mrs Midas' from *The World's Wife* by Carol Ann Duffy. Used by permission of Macmillan, London, UK.
'Uncle Edward's Affliction' by Vernon Scannell. Used by permission of Methuen Publishing Ltd.
'The Singing Foot' by Spike Milligan. Used by permission of Spike Milligan Productions Ltd.
Housekeeping by Marilynn Robinson. Used by permission of Faber and Faber Ltd.
Warlands by Rachel Anderson. Used by permission of Oxford University Press.
Moby Dick by Geraldine McCaughrean. Used by permission of Oxford University Press.
The Amber Spyglass by Philip Pullman, published 2000. Used by permission of Scholastic Ltd.
'Crossing Over' by Catherine Storr. Used by permission of The Peters Fraser and Dunlop Group.
'The Kitchen' from *Counting Stars* by David Almond. Used by permission of Hodder and Stoughton Limited.
The Big Sleep by Raymond Chandler. Used by permission of Penguin UK.
'Happy calf' from *Moortown Diaries* by Ted Hughes. Used by permission of Faber and Faber Ltd.
Top Girls by Caryl Churchill. Used by permission of Methuen Publishing Ltd.

Every effort has been made to trace copyright holders and to obtain their permission for the use of copyright material. The author and publishers will gladly receive information enabling them to rectify any error or omission in subsequent editions.